THE GREAT GATSBY

F. Scott Fitzgerald

SPARK PUBLISHING

*spark notes

© 2002, 2007 SparkNotes LLC
This 2014 edition printed for SparkNotes LLC by Sterling Publishing Co., Inc.

ISBN 978-1-4114-6957-0

Distributed in Canada by Sterling Publishing Co., Inc.
c/o Canadian Manda Group, 664 Annette Street
Toronto, Ontario M6S 2C8, Canada
Distributed in the United Kingdom by GMC Distribution Services
Castle Place, 166 High Street, Lewes, East Sussex BN7 1XU, England
Distributed in Australia by NewSouth Books
University of New South Wales, Sydney, NSW 2052, Australia

For information about custom editions, special sales, and premium and corporate
purchases, please contact Sterling Special Sales at specialsales@sterlingpublishing.com.

Manufactured in Canada

Lot #:
18 20 19 17
12/22

sparknotes.com
sterlingpublishing.com

Please email content@sparknotes.com to report any errors.

CONTENTS

CONTEXT

FRANCIS SCOTT KEY FITZGERALD was born on September 24, 1896, and named after his ancestor Francis Scott Key, the author of "The Star-Spangled Banner." Fitzgerald was raised in St. Paul, Minnesota. Though an intelligent child, he did poorly in school and was sent to a New Jersey boarding school in 1911. Despite being a mediocre student there, he managed to enroll at Princeton in 1913. Academic troubles and apathy plagued him throughout his time at college, and he never graduated, instead enlisting in the army in 1917, as World War I neared its end.

Fitzgerald became a second lieutenant, and was stationed at Camp Sheridan, in Montgomery, Alabama. There he met and fell in love with a wild seventeen-year-old beauty named Zelda Sayre. Zelda finally agreed to marry him, but her overpowering desire for wealth, fun, and leisure led her to delay their wedding until he could prove a success. With the publication of *This Side of Paradise* in 1920, Fitzgerald became a literary sensation, earning enough money and fame to convince Zelda to marry him.

Many of these events from Fitzgerald's early life appear in his most famous novel, *The Great Gatsby,* published in 1925. Like Fitzgerald, Nick Carraway is a thoughtful young man from Minnesota, educated at an Ivy League school (in Nick's case, Yale), who moves to New York after the war. Also similar to Fitzgerald is Jay Gatsby, a sensitive young man who idolizes wealth and luxury and who falls in love with a beautiful young woman while stationed at a military camp in the South.

Having become a celebrity, Fitzgerald fell into a wild, reckless life-style of parties and decadence, while desperately trying to please Zelda by writing to earn money. Similarly, Gatsby amasses a great deal of wealth at a relatively young age, and devotes himself to acquiring possessions and throwing parties that he believes will enable him to win Daisy's love. As the giddiness of the Roaring Twenties dissolved into the bleakness of the Great Depression, however, Zelda suffered a nervous breakdown and Fitzgerald battled alcoholism, which hampered his writing. He published *Tender Is the Night* in 1934, and sold short stories to *The Saturday Evening Post* to support his lavish lifestyle. In 1937, he left for Hollywood to write screenplays, and in 1940, while working on his novel *The Love of the Last Tycoon,* died of a heart attack at the age of forty-four.

Fitzgerald was the most famous chronicler of 1920s America, an era that he dubbed "the Jazz Age." Written in 1925, *The Great Gatsby* is one of the greatest literary documents of this period, in which the American economy soared, bringing unprecedented levels of prosperity to the nation. Prohibition, the ban on the sale and consumption of alcohol mandated by the Eighteenth Amendment to the Constitution (1919), made millionaires out of bootleggers, and an underground culture of revelry sprang up. Sprawling private parties managed to elude police notice, and "speakeasies"—secret clubs that sold liquor—thrived. The chaos and violence of World War I left America in a state of shock, and the generation that fought the war turned to wild and extravagant living to compensate. The staid conservatism and timeworn values of the previous decade were turned on their ear, as money, opulence, and exuberance became the order of the day.

Like Nick in *The Great Gatsby,* Fitzgerald found this new lifestyle seductive and exciting, and, like Gatsby, he had always idolized the very rich. Now he found himself in an era in which unrestrained materialism set the tone of society, particularly in the large cities of the East. Even so, like Nick, Fitzgerald saw through the glitter of the Jazz Age to the moral emptiness and hypocrisy beneath, and part of him longed for this absent moral center. In many ways, *The Great Gatsby* represents Fitzgerald's attempt to confront his conflicting feelings about the Jazz Age. Like Gatsby, Fitzgerald was driven by his love for a woman who symbolized everything he wanted, even as she led him toward everything he despised.

Plot Overview

ICK CARRAWAY, A YOUNG MAN from Minnesota, moves to New York in the summer of 1922 to learn about the bond business. He rents a house in the West Egg district of Long Island, a wealthy but un-fashionable area populated by the new rich, a group who have made their fortunes too recently to have established social connections and who are prone to garish displays of wealth. Nick's next-door neighbor in West Egg is a mysterious man named Jay Gatsby, who lives in a gigantic Gothic mansion and throws extravagant parties every Saturday night.

Nick is unlike the other inhabitants of West Egg—he was educated at Yale and has social connections in East Egg, a fashionable area of Long Island home to the established upper class. Nick drives out to East Egg one evening for dinner with his cousin, Daisy Buchanan, and her husband, Tom, an erstwhile classmate of Nick's at Yale. Daisy and Tom introduce Nick to Jordan Baker, a beautiful, cynical young woman with whom Nick begins a romantic relationship. Nick also learns a bit about Daisy and Tom's marriage: Jordan tells him that Tom has a lover, Myrtle Wilson, who lives in the valley of ashes, a gray industrial dumping ground between West Egg and New York City. Not long after this revelation, Nick travels to New York City with Tom and Myrtle. At a vulgar, gaudy party in the apartment that Tom keeps for the affair, Myrtle begins to taunt Tom about Daisy, and Tom responds by breaking her nose.

As the summer progresses, Nick eventually garners an invitation to one of Gatsby's legendary parties. He encounters Jordan Baker at the party, and they meet Gatsby himself, a surprisingly young man who affects an English accent, has a remarkable smile, and calls everyone "old sport." Gatsby asks to speak to Jordan alone, and, through Jordan, Nick later learns more about his mysterious neighbor. Gatsby tells Jordan that he knew Daisy in Louisville in 1917 and is deeply in love with her. He spends many nights staring at the green light at the end of her dock, across the bay from his mansion. Gatsby's extravagant lifestyle and wild parties are simply an attempt to impress Daisy. Gatsby now wants Nick to arrange a reunion between himself and Daisy, but he is afraid that Daisy will refuse to see him if she knows that he still loves her. Nick invites Daisy to have tea at his house, without telling her that Gatsby will also be there. After an initially awkward reunion, Gatsby and Daisy reestablish their connection. Their love rekindled, they begin an affair.

After a short time, Tom grows increasingly suspicious of his wife's relationship with Gatsby. At a luncheon at the Buchanans' house, Gatsby stares at Daisy with such undisguised passion that Tom realizes Gatsby is in love with her. Though Tom is himself involved in an extramarital affair, he is deeply outraged by the thought that his wife could be unfaithful to him. He forces the group to drive into New York City, where he confronts Gatsby in a suite at the Plaza Hotel. Tom asserts that he and Daisy have a history that Gatsby could never understand, and he announces to his wife that Gatsby is a criminal—his fortune comes from bootlegging alcohol and other illegal activities. Daisy realizes that her allegiance is to Tom, and Tom contemptuously sends her back to East Egg with Gatsby, attempting to prove that Gatsby cannot hurt him.

When Nick, Jordan, and Tom drive through the valley of ashes, however, they discover that Gatsby's car has struck and killed Myrtle, Tom's lover. They rush back to Long Island, where Nick learns from Gatsby that Daisy was driving the car when it struck Myrtle, but that Gatsby intends to take the blame. The next day, Tom tells Myrtle's husband, George, that Gatsby was the driver of the car. George, who has leapt to the conclusion that the driver of the car that killed Myrtle must have been her lover, finds Gatsby in the pool at his mansion and shoots him dead. He then fatally shoots himself.

Nick stages a small funeral for Gatsby, ends his relationship with Jordan, and moves back to the Midwest to escape the disgust he feels for the people surrounding Gatsby's life and for the emptiness and moral decay of life among the wealthy on the East Coast. Nick reflects that just as Gatsby's dream of Daisy was corrupted by money and dishonesty, the American dream of happiness and individualism has disintegrated into the mere pursuit of wealth. Though Gatsby's power to transform his dreams into reality is what makes him "great," Nick reflects that the era of dreaming—both Gatsby's dream and the American dream—is over.

Character List

Nick Carraway The novel's narrator, Nick is a young man from Minnesota who, after being educated at Yale and fighting in World War I, goes to New York City to learn the bond business. Honest, tolerant, and inclined to reserve judgment, Nick often serves as a confidant for those with troubling secrets. After moving to West Egg, a fictional area of Long Island that is home to the newly rich, Nick quickly befriends his next-door neighbor, the mysterious Jay Gatsby. As Daisy Buchanan's cousin, he facilitates the rekindling of the romance between her and Gatsby. *The Great Gatsby* is told entirely through Nick's eyes; his thoughts and perceptions shape and color the story.

Jay Gatsby The title character and protagonist of the novel, Gatsby is a fabulously wealthy young man living in a Gothic mansion in West Egg. He is famous for the lavish parties he throws every Saturday night, but no one knows where he comes from, what he does, or how he made his fortune. As the novel progresses, Nick learns that Gatsby was born James Gatz on a farm in North Dakota; working for a millionaire made him dedicate his life to the achievement of wealth. When he met Daisy while training to be an officer in Louisville, he fell in love with her. Nick also learns that Gatsby made his fortune through criminal activity, as he was willing to do anything to gain the social position he thought necessary to win Daisy. Nick views Gatsby as a deeply flawed man, dishonest and vulgar, whose extraordinary optimism and power to transform his dreams into reality make him "great" nonetheless.

Daisy Buchanan Nick's cousin, and the woman Gatsby loves. As a young woman in Louisville before the war, Daisy was courted by a number of officers, including Gatsby. She fell in love with Gatsby and promised to wait for him. However, Daisy harbors a deep need

5

to be loved, and when a wealthy, powerful young man named Tom Buchanan asked her to marry him, Daisy decided not to wait for Gatsby after all. Now a beautiful socialite, Daisy lives with Tom across from Gatsby in the fashionable East Egg district of Long Island. She is sardonic and somewhat cynical, and behaves superficially to mask her pain at her husband's constant infidelity.

Tom Buchanan Daisy's immensely wealthy husband, once a member of Nick's social club at Yale. Powerfully built and hailing from a socially solid old family, Tom is an arrogant, hypocritical bully. His social attitudes are laced with racism and sexism, and he never even considers trying to live up to the moral standard he demands from those around him. He has no moral qualms about his own extramarital affair with Myrtle, but when he begins to suspect Daisy and Gatsby of having an affair, he becomes outraged and forces a confrontation.

Jordan Baker Daisy's friend, a woman with whom Nick becomes romantically involved during the course of the novel. A competitive golfer, Jordan represents one of the "new women" of the 1920s—cynical, boyish, and self-centered. Jordan is beautiful, but also dishonest: she cheated in order to win her first golf tournament and continually bends the truth.

Myrtle Wilson Tom's lover, whose lifeless husband George owns a run-down garage in the valley of ashes. Myrtle herself possesses a fierce vitality and desperately looks for a way to improve her situation. Unfortunately for her, she chooses Tom, who treats her as a mere object of his desire.

George Wilson Myrtle's husband, the lifeless, exhausted owner of a run-down auto shop at the edge of the valley of ashes. George loves and idealizes Myrtle, and is devastated by her affair with Tom. George is consumed with grief when Myrtle is killed. George is comparable to Gatsby in that both are dreamers and both are ruined by their unrequited love for women who love Tom.

Owl Eyes   The eccentric, bespectacled drunk whom Nick meets at the first party he attends at Gatsby's mansion. Nick finds Owl Eyes looking through Gatsby's library, astonished that the books are real.

Klipspringer   The shallow freeloader who seems almost to live at Gatsby's mansion, taking advantage of his host's money. As soon as Gatsby dies, Klipspringer disappears—he does not attend the funeral, but he does call Nick about a pair of tennis shoes that he left at Gatsby's mansion.

CHARACTER LIST

ANALYSIS OF MAJOR CHARACTERS

JAY GATSBY

The title character of *The Great Gatsby* is a young man, around thirty years old, who rose from an impoverished childhood in rural North Dakota to become fabulously wealthy. However, he achieved this lofty goal by participating in organized crime, including distributing illegal alcohol and trading in stolen securities. From his early youth, Gatsby despised poverty and longed for wealth and sophistication—he dropped out of St. Olaf's College after only two weeks because he could not bear the janitorial job with which he was paying his tuition. Though Gatsby has always wanted to be rich, his main motivation in acquiring his fortune was his love for Daisy Buchanan, whom he met as a young military officer in Louisville before leaving to fight in World War I in 1917. Gatsby immediately fell in love with Daisy's aura of luxury, grace, and charm, and lied to her about his own background in order to convince her that he was good enough for her. Daisy promised to wait for him when he left for the war, but married Tom Buchanan in 1919, while Gatsby was studying at Oxford after the war in an attempt to gain an education. From that moment on, Gatsby dedicated himself to winning Daisy back, and his acquisition of millions of dollars, his purchase of a gaudy mansion on West Egg, and his lavish weekly parties are all merely means to that end.

Fitzgerald delays the introduction of most of this information until fairly late in the novel. Gatsby's reputation precedes him— Gatsby himself does not appear in a speaking role until Chapter III. Fitzgerald initially presents Gatsby as the aloof, enigmatic host of the unbelievably opulent parties thrown every week at his mansion. He appears surrounded by spectacular luxury, courted by powerful men and beautiful women. He is the subject of a whirlwind of gossip throughout New York and is already a kind of legendary celebrity before he is ever introduced to the reader. Fitzgerald propels the novel forward through the early chapters by shrouding Gatsby's background and the source of his wealth in mystery (the reader learns about Gatsby's childhood in Chapter VI and receives definitive proof of his criminal dealings in Chapter VII). As a result, the reader's first, distant impressions of Gatsby strike quite a different note from that of the lovesick, naive young man who emerges during the later part of the novel.

Fitzgerald uses this technique of delayed character revelation to emphasize the theatrical quality of Gatsby's approach to life, which is an important part of his personality. Gatsby has literally created his own character, even changing his name from James Gatz to Jay Gatsby to represent his reinvention of himself. As his relentless quest for Daisy demonstrates, Gatsby has an extraordinary ability to transform his hopes and dreams into reality; at the beginning of the novel, he appears to the reader just as he desires to appear to the world. This talent for self-invention is what gives Gatsby his quality of "greatness": indeed, the title "*The Great Gatsby*" is reminiscent of billings for such vaudeville magicians as "The Great Houdini" and "The Great Blackstone," suggesting that the persona of Jay Gatsby is a masterful illusion.

> *Gatsby believed in the green light, the orgastic future that year by year recedes before us.*
>
> *(See* QUOTATIONS, *p. 45)*

As the novel progresses and Fitzgerald deconstructs Gatsby's self-presentation, Gatsby reveals himself to be an innocent, hopeful young man who stakes everything on his dreams, not realizing that his dreams are unworthy of him. Gatsby invests Daisy with an idealistic perfection that she cannot possibly attain in reality and pursues her with a passionate zeal that blinds him to her limitations. His dream of her disintegrates, revealing the corruption that wealth causes and the unworthiness of the goal, much in the way Fitzgerald sees the American dream crumbling in the 1920s, as America's powerful optimism, vitality, and individualism become subordinated to the amoral pursuit of wealth.

Gatsby is contrasted most consistently with Nick. Critics point out that the former, passionate and active, and the latter, sober and reflective, seem to represent two sides of Fitzgerald's personality. Additionally, whereas Tom is a cold-hearted, aristocratic bully, Gatsby is a loyal and good-hearted man. Though his lifestyle and attitude differ greatly from those of George Wilson, Gatsby and Wilson share the fact that they both lose their love interest to Tom.

CHARACTER ANALYSIS

NICK CARRAWAY

If Gatsby represents one part of Fitzgerald's personality, the flashy celebrity who pursued and glorified wealth in order to impress the woman he loved, then Nick represents another part: the quiet, reflective Midwesterner adrift in the lurid East. A young man (he turns thirty during the course of the novel) from Minnesota, Nick travels to New York in 1922 to learn the bond business. He lives in the West Egg district of Long Island, next door to Gatsby. Nick is also Daisy's cousin, which enables him to observe and assist the resurgent love affair between Daisy and Gatsby. As a result of his relationship to these two characters, Nick is the perfect choice to narrate the novel, which functions as a personal memoir of his experiences with Gatsby in the summer of 1922.

Nick is also well suited to narrating *The Great Gatsby* because of his temperament. As he tells the reader in Chapter I, he is tolerant, open-minded, quiet, and a good listener, and, as a result, others tend to talk to him and tell him their secrets. Gatsby, in particular, comes to trust him and treat him as a confidant. Nick generally assumes a secondary role throughout the novel, preferring to describe and comment on events rather than dominate the action. Often, however, he functions as Fitzgerald's voice, as in his extended meditation on time and the American dream at the end of Chapter IX.

Insofar as Nick plays a role inside the narrative, he evidences a strongly mixed reaction to life on the East Coast, one that creates a powerful internal conflict that he does not resolve until the end of the book. On the one hand, Nick is attracted to the fast-paced, fun-driven lifestyle of New York. On the other hand, he finds that lifestyle grotesque and damaging. This inner conflict is symbolized throughout the book by Nick's romantic affair with Jordan Baker. He is attracted to her vivacity and her sophistication just as he is repelled by her dishonesty and her lack of consideration for other people.

Nick states that there is a "quality of distortion" to life in New York, and this lifestyle makes him lose his equilibrium, especially early in the novel, as when he gets drunk at Gatsby's party in Chapter II. After witnessing the unraveling of Gatsby's dream and presiding over the appalling spectacle of Gatsby's funeral, Nick realizes that the fast life of revelry on the East Coast is a cover for the terrifying moral emptiness that the valley of ashes symbolizes. Having gained the maturity that this insight demonstrates, he returns to Minnesota in search of a quieter life structured by more traditional moral values.

DAISY BUCHANAN

Partially based on Fitzgerald's wife, Zelda, Daisy is a beautiful young woman from Louisville, Kentucky. She is Nick's cousin and the object of Gatsby's love. As a young debutante in Louisville, Daisy was extremely popular among the military officers stationed near her home, including Jay Gatsby. Gatsby lied about his background to Daisy, claiming to be from a wealthy family in order to convince her that he was worthy of her. Eventually, Gatsby won Daisy's heart, and they made love before Gatsby left to fight in the war. Daisy promised to wait for Gatsby, but in 1919 she chose instead to marry Tom Buchanan, a young man from a solid, aristocratic family who could promise her a wealthy lifestyle and who had the support of her parents.

After 1919, Gatsby dedicated himself to winning Daisy back, making her the single goal of all of his dreams and the main motivation behind his acquisition of immense wealth through criminal activity. To Gatsby, Daisy represents the paragon of perfection—she has the aura of charm, wealth, sophistication, grace, and aristocracy that he longed for as a child in North Dakota and that first attracted him to her. In reality, however, Daisy falls far short of Gatsby's ideals. She is beautiful and charming, but also fickle, shallow, bored, and sardonic. Nick characterizes her as a careless person who smashes things up and then retreats behind her money. Daisy proves her real nature when she chooses Tom over Gatsby in Chapter VII, then allows Gatsby to take the blame for killing Myrtle Wilson even though she herself was driving the car. Finally, rather than attend Gatsby's funeral, Daisy and Tom move away, leaving no forwarding address.

Like Zelda Fitzgerald, Daisy is in love with money, ease, and material luxury. She is capable of affection (she seems genuinely fond of Nick and occasionally seems to love Gatsby sincerely), but not of sustained loyalty or care. She is indifferent even to her own infant daughter, never discussing her and treating her as an afterthought when she is introduced in Chapter VII. In Fitzgerald's conception of America in the 1920s, Daisy represents the amoral values of the aristocratic East Egg set.

Themes, Motifs & Symbols

Themes

Themes are the fundamental and often universal ideas explored in a literary work.

The Decline of the American Dream in the 1920s

On the surface, *The Great Gatsby* is a story of the thwarted love between a man and a woman. The main theme of the novel, however, encompasses a much larger, less romantic scope. Though all of its action takes place over a mere few months during the summer of 1922 and is set in a circumscribed geographical area in the vicinity of Long Island, New York, *The Great Gatsby* is a highly symbolic meditation on 1920s America as a whole, in particular the disintegration of the American dream in an era of unprecedented prosperity and material excess.

Fitzgerald portrays the 1920s as an era of decayed social and moral values, evidenced in its overarching cynicism, greed, and empty pursuit of pleasure. The reckless jubilance that led to decadent parties and wild jazz music—epitomized in *The Great Gatsby* by the opulent parties that Gatsby throws every Saturday night—resulted ultimately in the corruption of the American dream, as the unrestrained desire for money and pleasure surpassed more noble goals. When World War I ended in 1918, the generation of young Americans who had fought the war became intensely disillusioned, as the brutal carnage that they had just faced made the Victorian social morality of early-twentieth-century America seem like stuffy, empty hypocrisy. The dizzying rise of the stock market in the aftermath of the war led to a sudden, sustained increase in the national wealth and a newfound materialism, as people began to spend and consume at unprecedented levels. A person from any social background could, potentially, make a fortune, but the American aristocracy—families with old wealth—scorned the newly rich industrialists and speculators. Additionally, the passage of the Eighteenth Amendment in 1919, which banned the sale of alcohol, created a thriving underworld designed to satisfy the massive demand for bootleg liquor among rich and poor alike.

Fitzgerald positions the characters of *The Great Gatsby* as emblems of these social trends. Nick and Gatsby, both of whom fought in World War I, exhibit the newfound cosmopolitanism and cynicism that resulted from the war. The various social climbers and ambitious speculators who attend Gatsby's parties evidence the greedy scramble for wealth. The clash between "old money" and "new money" manifests itself in the novel's symbolic geography: East Egg represents the established aristocracy, West Egg the self-made rich. Meyer Wolfshiem and Gatsby's fortune symbolize the rise of organized crime and bootlegging.

As Fitzgerald saw it (and as Nick explains in Chapter IX), the American dream was originally about discovery, individualism, and the pursuit of happiness. In the 1920s depicted in the novel, however, easy money and relaxed social values have corrupted this dream, especially on the East Coast. The main plotline of the novel reflects this assessment, as Gatsby's dream of loving Daisy is ruined by the difference in their respective social statuses, his resorting to crime to make enough money to impress her, and the rampant materialism that characterizes her lifestyle. Additionally, places and objects in *The Great Gatsby* have meaning only because characters instill them with meaning: the eyes of Doctor T. J. Eckleburg best exemplify this idea. In Nick's mind, the ability to create meaningful symbols constitutes a central component of the American dream, as early Americans invested their new nation with their own ideals and values.

Nick compares the green bulk of America rising from the ocean to the green light at the end of Daisy's dock. Just as Americans have given America meaning through their dreams for their own lives, Gatsby instills Daisy with a kind of idealized perfection that she neither deserves nor possesses. Gatsby's dream is ruined by the unworthiness of its object, just as the American dream in the 1920s is ruined by the unworthiness of its object—money and pleasure. Like 1920s Americans in general, fruitlessly seeking a bygone era in which their dreams had value, Gatsby longs to re-create a vanished past—his time in Louisville with Daisy—but is incapable of doing so. When his dream crumbles, all that is left for Gatsby to do is die; all Nick can do is move back to Minnesota, where American values have not decayed.

THE HOLLOWNESS OF THE UPPER CLASS

One of the major topics explored in *The Great Gatsby* is the sociology of wealth, specifically, how the newly minted millionaires of the 1920s differ from and relate to the old aristocracy of the country's richest families. In the novel, West Egg and its denizens represent the newly rich, while East Egg and its denizens, especially Daisy and Tom, represent the old aristocracy. Fitzgerald portrays the newly rich as being vulgar, gaudy, ostentatious, and lacking in social graces and taste. Gatsby, for example, lives in a monstrously ornate mansion, wears a pink suit, drives a Rolls-Royce, and does not pick up on subtle social signals, such as the insincerity of the Sloanes' invitation to lunch. In contrast, the old aristocracy possesses grace, taste, subtlety, and elegance, epitomized by the Buchanans' tasteful home and the flowing white dresses of Daisy and Jordan Baker.

What the old aristocracy possesses in taste, however, it seems to lack in heart, as the East Eggers prove themselves careless, inconsiderate bullies who are so used to money's ability to ease their minds that they never worry about hurting others. The Buchanans exemplify this stereotype when, at the end of the novel, they simply move to a new house far away rather than condescend to attend Gatsby's funeral. Gatsby, on the other hand, whose recent wealth derives from criminal activity, has a sincere and loyal heart, remaining outside Daisy's window until four in the morning in Chapter VII simply to make sure that Tom does not hurt her. Ironically, Gatsby's good qualities (loyalty and love) lead to his death, as he takes the blame for killing Myrtle rather than letting Daisy be punished, and the Buchanans' bad qualities (fickleness and selfishness) allow them to remove themselves from the tragedy not only physically but psychologically.

MOTIFS

Motifs are recurring structures, contrasts, and literary devices that can help to develop and inform the text's major themes.

GEOGRAPHY

Throughout the novel, places and settings epitomize the various aspects of the 1920s American society that Fitzgerald depicts. East Egg represents the old aristocracy, West Egg the newly rich, the valley of ashes the moral and social decay of America, and New York City the uninhibited, amoral quest for money and pleasure. Additionally, the East is connected to the moral decay and social cynicism of New York, while the West (including Midwestern and northern areas such as Minnesota) is connected to more traditional social values and ideals. Nick's analysis in Chapter IX of the story he has related reveals his sensitivity to this dichotomy: though it is set in the East, the story is really one of the West, as it tells how people originally from west of the Appalachians (as all of the main characters are) react to the pace and style of life on the East Coast.

WEATHER

As in much of Shakespeare's work, the weather in *The Great Gatsby* unfailingly matches the emotional and narrative tone of the story. Gatsby and Daisy's reunion begins amid a pouring rain, proving awkward and melancholy; their love reawakens just as the sun begins to come out. Gatsby's climactic confrontation with Tom occurs on the hottest day of the summer, under the scorching sun (like the fatal encounter between Mercutio and Tybalt in Romeo and Juliet). Wilson kills Gatsby on the first day of autumn, as Gatsby floats in his pool despite a palpable chill in the air—a symbolic attempt to stop time and restore his relationship with Daisy to the way it was five years before, in 1917.

SYMBOLS

Symbols are objects, characters, figures, and colors used to represent abstract ideas or concepts.

THE GREEN LIGHT

Situated at the end of Daisy's East Egg dock and barely visible from Gatsby's West Egg lawn, the green light represents Gatsby's hopes and dreams for the future. Gatsby associates it with Daisy, and in Chapter I he reaches toward it in the darkness as a guiding light to lead him to his goal. Because Gatsby's quest for Daisy is broadly associated with the American dream, the green light also symbolizes that more generalized ideal. In Chapter IX, Nick compares the green light to how America, rising out of the ocean, must have looked to early settlers of the new nation.

THE VALLEY OF ASHES

First introduced in Chapter II, the valley of ashes between West Egg and New York City consists of a long stretch of desolate land created by the dumping of industrial ashes. It represents the moral and social decay that results from the uninhibited pursuit of wealth, as

SYMBOLS

the rich indulge themselves with regard for nothing but their own pleasure. The valley of ashes also symbolizes the plight of the poor, like George Wilson, who live among the dirty ashes and lose their vitality as a result.

The Eyes of Doctor T. J. Eckleburg

The eyes of Doctor T. J. Eckleburg are a pair of fading, bespectacled eyes painted on an old advertising billboard over the valley of ashes. They may represent God staring down upon and judging American society as a moral wasteland, though the novel never makes this point explicitly. Instead, throughout the novel, Fitzgerald suggests that symbols only have meaning because characters instill them with meaning. The connection between the eyes of Doctor T. J. Eckleburg and God exists only in George Wilson's grief-stricken mind. This lack of concrete significance contributes to the unsettling nature of the image. Thus, the eyes also come to represent the essential meaninglessness of the world and the arbitrariness of the mental process by which people invest objects with meaning. Nick explores these ideas in Chapter VIII, when he imagines Gatsby's final thoughts as a depressed consideration of the emptiness of symbols and dreams.

SUMMARY & ANALYSIS

CHAPTER I

SUMMARY

The narrator of *The Great Gatsby* is a young man from Minnesota named Nick Carraway. He not only narrates the story but casts himself as the book's author. He begins by commenting on himself, stating that he learned from his father to reserve judgment about other people, because if he holds them up to his own moral standards, he will misunderstand them. He characterizes himself as both highly moral and highly tolerant. He briefly mentions the hero of his story, Gatsby, saying that Gatsby represented everything he scorns, but that he exempts Gatsby completely from his usual judgments. Gatsby's personality was nothing short of "gorgeous."

In the summer of 1922, Nick writes, he had just arrived in New York, where he moved to work in the bond business, and rented a house on a part of Long Island called West Egg. Unlike the conservative, aristocratic East Egg, West Egg is home to the "new rich," those who, having made their fortunes recently, have neither the social connections nor the refinement to move among the East Egg set. West Egg is characterized by lavish displays of wealth and garish poor taste. Nick's comparatively modest West Egg house is next door to Gatsby's mansion, a sprawling Gothic monstrosity.

Nick is unlike his West Egg neighbors; whereas they lack social connections and aristocratic pedigrees, Nick graduated from Yale and has many connections on East Egg. One night, he drives out to East Egg to have dinner with his cousin Daisy and her husband, Tom Buchanan, a former member of Nick's social club at Yale. Tom, a powerful figure dressed in riding clothes, greets Nick on the porch. Inside, Daisy lounges on a couch with her friend Jordan Baker, a competitive golfer who yawns as though bored by her surroundings.

Tom tries to interest the others in a book called *The Rise of the Colored Empires* by a man named Goddard. The book espouses racist, white-supremacist attitudes that Tom seems to find convincing. Daisy teases Tom about the book but is interrupted when Tom leaves the room to take a phone call. Daisy follows him hurriedly, and Jordan tells Nick that the call is from Tom's lover in New York.

After an awkward dinner, the party breaks up. Jordan wants to go to bed because she has a golf tournament the next day. As Nick leaves, Tom and Daisy hint that they would like for him to take a romantic interest in Jordan.

When Nick arrives home, he sees Gatsby for the first time, a handsome young man standing on the lawn with his arms reaching out toward the dark water. Nick looks out at the water, but all he can see is a distant green light that might mark the end of a dock.

> *"I hope she'll be a fool—that's the best thing a girl can be in this world, a beautiful little fool."*
>
> (See QUOTATIONS, p. 41)

ANALYSIS

Nick Carraway's perceptions and attitudes regarding the events and characters of the novel are central to *The Great Gatsby*. Writing the novel is Nick's way of grappling with the meaning of a story in which he played a part. The first pages of Chapter I establish certain contradictions in Nick's point of view. Although he describes himself as tolerant and nonjudgmental, he also views himself as morally privileged, having a better sense of "decencies" than most other people. While Nick has a strong negative reaction to his experiences in New York and eventually returns to the Midwest in search of a less morally ambiguous environment, even during his initial phase of disgust, Gatsby stands out for him as an exception. Nick admires Gatsby highly, despite the fact that Gatsby represents everything Nick scorns about New York. Gatsby clearly poses a challenge to Nick's customary ways of thinking about the world, and Nick's struggle to come to terms with that challenge inflects everything in the novel.

In the world of East Egg, alluring appearances serve to cover unattractive realities. The marriage of Tom and Daisy Buchanan seems menaced by a quiet desperation beneath its pleasant surface. Unlike Nick, Tom is arrogant and dishonest, advancing racist arguments at dinner and carrying on relatively public love affairs. Daisy, on the other hand, tries hard to be shallow, even going so far as to say she hopes her baby daughter will turn out to be a fool, because women live best as beautiful fools. Jordan Baker furthers the sense of sophisticated fatigue hanging over East Egg: her cynicism, boredom, and dishonesty are at sharp odds with her wealth and beauty.

As with the Buchanans' marriage, Jordan's surface glamour covers up an inner emptiness.

Gatsby stands in stark contrast to the denizens of East Egg. Though Nick does not yet know the green light's origin, nor what it represents for Gatsby, the inner yearning visible in Gatsby's posture and his emotional surrender to it make him seem almost the opposite of the sarcastic Ivy League set at the Buchanans'. Gatsby is a mysterious figure for Nick, since Nick knows neither his motives, nor the source of his wealth, nor his history, and the object of his yearning remains as remote and nebulous as the green light toward which he reaches.

The relationship between geography and social values is an important motif in *The Great Gatsby*. Each setting in the novel corresponds to a particular thematic idea or character type. This first chapter introduces two of the most important locales, East Egg and West Egg. Though each is home to fabulous wealth, and though they are separated only by a small expanse of water, the two regions are nearly opposite in the values they endorse. East Egg represents breeding, taste, aristocracy, and leisure, while West Egg represents ostentation, garishness, and the flashy manners of the new rich. East Egg is associated with the Buchanans and the monotony of their inherited social position, while West Egg is associated with Gatsby's gaudy mansion and the inner drive behind his self-made fortune. The unworkable intersection of the two Eggs in the romance between Gatsby and Daisy will serve as the fault line of catastrophe.

CHAPTER II

SUMMARY

Halfway between West Egg and New York City sprawls a desolate plain, a gray valley where New York's ashes are dumped. The men who live here work at shoveling up the ashes. Overhead, two huge, blue, spectacle-rimmed eyes—the last vestige of an advertising gimmick by a long-vanished eye doctor—stare down from an enormous sign. These unblinking eyes, the eyes of Doctor T. J. Eckleburg, watch over everything that happens in the valley of ashes.

The commuter train that runs between West Egg and New York passes through the valley, making several stops along the way. One day, as Nick and Tom are riding the train into the city, Tom forces Nick to follow him out of the train at one of these stops. Tom leads Nick to George Wilson's garage, which sits on the edge of the valley of ashes. Tom's lover Myrtle is Wilson's wife. Wilson is a lifeless yet handsome man, colored gray by the ashes in the air. In contrast, Myrtle has a kind of desperate vitality; she strikes Nick as sensuous despite her stocky figure. Tom taunts Wilson and then orders Myrtle to follow him to the train. Tom takes Nick and Myrtle to New York City, to the Morningside Heights apartment he keeps for his affair. Here they have an impromptu party with Myrtle's sister, Catherine, and a couple named McKee. Catherine has bright red hair, wears a great deal of makeup, and tells Nick that she has heard that Jay Gatsby is the nephew or cousin of Kaiser Wilhelm, the ruler of Germany during World War I. The McKees, who live downstairs, are a horrid couple: Mr. McKee is pale and feminine, and Mrs. McKee is shrill. The group proceeds to drink excessively. Nick claims that he got drunk for only the second time in his life at this party.

The ostentatious behavior and conversation of the others at the party repulse Nick, and he tries to leave. At the same time, he finds himself fascinated by the lurid spectacle of the group. Myrtle grows louder and more obnoxious the more she drinks, and shortly after Tom gives her a new puppy as a gift, she begins to talk about Daisy. Tom sternly warns her never to mention his wife. Myrtle angrily says that she will talk about whatever she chooses and begins chanting Daisy's name. Tom responds by breaking her nose, bringing the party to an abrupt halt. Nick leaves, drunkenly, with Mr. McKee, and ends up taking the 4 A.M. train back to Long Island.

ANALYSIS

Unlike the other settings in the book, the valley of ashes is a picture of absolute desolation and poverty. It lacks a glamorous surface and lies fallow and gray halfway between West Egg and New York. The valley of ashes symbolizes the moral decay hidden by the beautiful facades of the Eggs, and suggests that beneath the ornamentation of West Egg and the mannered charm of East Egg lies the same ugliness as in the valley. The valley is created by industrial dumping and is therefore a by-product of capitalism. It is the home to the only poor characters in the novel.

The undefined significance of Doctor T. J. Eckleburg's monstrous, bespectacled eyes gazing down from their billboard makes them troubling to the reader: in this chapter, Fitzgerald preserves their mystery, giving them no fixed symbolic value. Enigmatically, the eyes simply "brood on over the solemn dumping ground." Perhaps the most persuasive reading of the eyes at this point in the novel is that they represent the eyes of God, staring down at the moral decay of the 1920s. The faded paint of the eyes can be seen as symbolizing the extent to which humanity has lost its connection to God. This reading, however, is merely suggested by the arrangement of the novel's symbols; Nick does not directly explain the symbol in this way, leaving the reader to interpret it.

The fourth and final setting of the novel, New York City, is in every way the opposite of the valley of ashes—it is loud, garish, abundant, and glittering. To Nick, New York is simultaneously fascinating and repulsive, thrillingly fast-paced and dazzling to look at but lacking a moral center. While Tom is forced to keep his affair with Myrtle relatively discreet in the valley of the ashes, in New York he can appear with her in public, even among his acquaintances, without causing a scandal. Even Nick, despite being Daisy's cousin, seems not to mind that Tom parades his infidelity in public.

The sequence of events leading up to and occurring at the party define and contrast the various characters in *The Great Gatsby*. Nick's reserved nature and indecisiveness show in the fact that though he feels morally repelled by the vulgarity and tastelessness of the party, he is too fascinated by it to leave. This contradiction suggests the ambivalence that he feels toward the Buchanans, Gatsby, and the East Coast in general. The party also underscores Tom's hypocrisy and lack of restraint: he feels no guilt for betraying Daisy with Myrtle, but he feels compelled to keep Myrtle in her place. Tom emerges in this section as a boorish bully who uses his social status and physical strength to dominate those around him—he subtly taunts Wilson while having an affair with his wife, experiences no guilt for his immoral behavior, and does not hesitate to lash out violently in order to preserve his authority over Myrtle. Wilson stands in stark contrast, a handsome and morally upright man who lacks money, privilege, and vitality.

Fitzgerald also uses the party scene to continue building an aura of mystery and excitement around Gatsby, who has yet to make a full appearance in the novel. Here, Gatsby emerges as a mysterious subject of gossip. He is extremely well known, but no one seems to have any verifiable information about him. The ridiculous rumor Catherine spreads shows the extent of the public's curiosity about him, rendering him more intriguing to both the other characters in the novel and the reader.

CHAPTER III

SUMMARY
One of the reasons that Gatsby has become so famous around New York is that he throws elaborate parties every weekend at his mansion, lavish spectacles to which people long to be invited. One day, Gatsby's chauffeur brings Nick an invitation to one of these parties. At the appointed time, Nick makes the short walk to Gatsby's house and joins the festivities, feeling somewhat out of place amid the throng of jubilant strangers. Guests mill around exchanging rumors about their host—no one seems to know the truth about Gatsby's wealth or personal history. Nick runs into Jordan Baker, whose friend, Lucille, speculates that Gatsby was a German spy during the war. Nick also hears that Gatsby is a graduate of Oxford and that he once killed a man in cold blood.

Gatsby's party is almost unbelievably luxurious: guests marvel over his Rolls-Royce, his swimming pool, his beach, crates of fresh oranges and lemons, buffet tents in the gardens overflowing with a feast, and a live orchestra playing under the stars. Liquor flows freely, and the crowd grows rowdier and louder as more and more guests get drunk. In this atmosphere of opulence and revelry, Nick and Jordan, curious about their host, set out to find Gatsby. Instead, they run into a middle-aged man with huge, owl-eyed spectacles (whom Nick dubs Owl Eyes) who sits poring over the unread books in Gatsby's library.

At midnight, Nick and Jordan go outside to watch the entertainment. They sit at a table with a handsome young man who says that Nick looks familiar to him; they realize that they served in the same division during the war. The man introduces himself as none other than Jay Gatsby. Gatsby's speech is elaborate and formal, and he has a habit of calling everyone "old sport." As the party progresses, Nick becomes increasingly fascinated with Gatsby. He notices that Gatsby does not drink and that he keeps himself separate from the party, standing alone on the marble steps, watching his guests in silence.

At two o'clock in the morning, as husbands and wives argue over whether to leave, a butler tells Jordan that Gatsby would like to see her. Jordan emerges from her meeting with Gatsby saying that she has just heard something extraordinary. Nick says goodbye to Gatsby, who goes inside to take a phone call from Philadelphia. Nick starts to walk home. On his way, he sees Owl Eyes struggling to get his car out of a ditch. Owl Eyes and another man climb out of the wrecked automobile, and Owl Eyes drunkenly declares that he washes his hands of the whole business.

Nick then proceeds to describe his everyday life, to prove that he does more with his time than simply attend parties. He works in New York City, through which he also takes long walks, and he meets women. After a brief relationship with a girl from Jersey City, Nick follows the advice of Daisy and Tom and begins seeing Jordan Baker. Nick says that Jordan is fundamentally a dishonest person; he even knows that she cheated in her first golf tournament. Nick feels attracted to her despite her dishonesty, even though he himself claims to be one of the few honest people he has ever known.

> *He had one of those rare smiles with a quality of*
> *eternal reassurance in it, that you may come across*
> *four or five times in life.*
>
> (See QUOTATIONS, p. 42)

ANALYSIS

At the beginning of this chapter, Gatsby's party brings 1920s wealth and glamour into full focus, showing the upper class at its most lavishly opulent. The rich, both socialites from East Egg and their coarser counterparts from West Egg, cavort without restraint. As his depiction of the differences between East Egg and West Egg evidences, Fitzgerald is fascinated with the social hierarchy and mood of America in the 1920s, when a large group of industrialists, speculators, and businessmen with brand-new fortunes joined the old, aristocratic families at the top of the economic ladder. The "new rich" lack the refinement, manners, and taste of the "old rich" but long to break into the polite society of the East Eggers. In this scenario, Gatsby is again an enigma—though he lives in a garishly ostentatious West Egg mansion, East Eggers freely attend his parties. Despite the tensions between the two groups, the blend of East and West Egg creates a distinctly American mood. While the Americans at the party possess a rough vitality, the Englishmen there are set off dramatically, seeming desperate and predatory, hoping to make connections that will make them rich.

Fitzgerald has delayed the introduction of the novel's most important figure—Gatsby himself—until the beginning of Chapter III. The reader has seen Gatsby from a distance, heard other characters talk about him, and listened to Nick's thoughts about him, but has not actually met him (nor has Nick). Chapter III is devoted to the introduction of Gatsby and the lavish, showy world he inhabits. Fitzgerald gives Gatsby a suitably grand entrance as the aloof host of a spectacularly decadent party. Despite this introduction, this chapter continues to heighten the sense of mystery and enigma that surrounds Gatsby, as the low profile he maintains seems curiously out of place with his lavish expenditures. Just as he stood alone on his lawn in Chapter I, he now stands outside the throng of plea-sure-seekers. In his first direct contact with Gatsby, Nick notices his extraordinary smile—"one of those rare smiles with a quality of eternal reassurance in it." Nick's impression of Gatsby emphasizes his optimism and vitality—something about him seems remarkably hopeful, and this belief in the brilliance of the future impresses Nick, even before he knows what future Gatsby envisions.

Many aspects of Gatsby's world are intriguing because they are slightly amiss—for instance, he seems to throw parties at which he knows none of his guests. His accent seems affected, and his habit of calling people "old sport" is hard to place. One of his guests, Owl Eyes, is surprised to find that his books are real and not just empty covers designed to create the appearance of a great library. The tone of Nick's narration suggests that many of the inhabit-ants of East Egg and West Egg use an outward show of opulence to cover up their inner corruption and moral decay, but Gatsby seems to use his opulence to mask something entirely different and perhaps more profound. From this chapter forward, the mystery of Jay Gatsby becomes the motivating question of the book, and the unraveling of Gatsby's character becomes one of its central mecha-nisms. One early clue to Gatsby's character in this chapter is his mysterious conversation with Jordan Baker. Though Nick does not know what Gatsby says to her, the fact that Jordan now knows something "remarkable" about Gatsby means that a part of the solution to the enigma of Gatsby is now loose among Nick's circle of acquaintances.

Chapter III also focuses on the gap between perception and real-ity. At the party, as he looks through Gatsby's books, Owl Eyes states that Gatsby has captured the effect of theater, a kind of mingling of honesty and dishonesty that characterizes Gatsby's approach to this dimension of his life. The party itself is a kind of elaborate theatri-cal presentation, and Owl Eyes suggests that Gatsby's whole life is merely a show, believing that even his books might not be real. The novel's title itself—*The Great Gatsby*—is suggestive of the sort of vaudeville billing for a performer or magician like "The Great

Houdini," subtly emphasizing the theatrical and perhaps illusory quality of Gatsby's life.

Nick's description of his life in New York likewise calls attention to the difference between substance and appearance, as it emphasizes both the colorful allure of the city and its dangerous lack of balance: he says that the city has an "adventurous feel," but he also calls it "racy," a word with negative moral connotations. Nick feels similarly conflicted about Jordan. He realizes that she is dishonest, selfish, and cynical, but he is attracted to her vitality nevertheless. Their budding relationship emphasizes the extent to which Nick becomes acclimated to life in the East, abandoning his Midwestern values and concerns in order to take advantage of the excitement of his new surroundings.

CHAPTER IV

SUMMARY

Nick lists all of the people who attended Gatsby's parties that summer, a roll call of the nation's most wealthy and powerful people. He then describes a trip that he took to New York with Gatsby to eat lunch. As they drive to the city, Gatsby tells Nick about his past, but his story seems highly improbable. He claims, for instance, to be the son of wealthy, deceased parents from the Midwest. When Nick asks which Midwestern city he is from, Gatsby replies, "San Francisco." Gatsby then lists a long and preposterously detailed set of accomplishments: he claims to have been educated at Oxford, to have collected jewels in the capitals of Europe, to have hunted big game, and to have been awarded medals in World War I by multiple European countries. Seeing Nick's skepticism, Gatsby produces a medal from Montenegro and a picture of himself playing cricket at Oxford.

Gatsby's car speeds through the valley of ashes and enters the city. When a policeman pulls Gatsby over for speeding, Gatsby shows him a white card and the policeman apologizes for bothering him. In the city, Gatsby takes Nick to lunch and introduces him to Meyer Wolfshiem, who, he claims, was responsible for fixing the 1919 World Series. Wolfshiem is a shady character with underground business connections. He gives Nick the impression that the source of Gatsby's wealth might be unsavory, and that Gatsby may even have ties to the sort of organized crime with which Wolfshiem is associated.

After the lunch in New York, Nick sees Jordan Baker, who finally tells him the details of her mysterious conversation with Gatsby at the party. She relates that Gatsby told her that he is in love with Daisy Buchanan. According to Jordan, during the war, before Daisy married Tom, she was a beautiful young girl in Louisville, Kentucky, and all the military officers in town were in love with her. Daisy fell in love with Lieutenant Jay Gatsby, who was stationed at the base near her home. Though she chose to marry Tom after Gatsby left for the war, Daisy drank herself into numbness the night before her wedding, after she received a letter from Gatsby. Daisy has apparently remained faithful to her husband throughout their marriage, but Tom has not. Jordan adds that Gatsby bought his mansion in West Egg solely to be near Daisy. Nick remembers the night he saw Gatsby stretching his arms out to the water and realizes that the green light he saw was the light at the end of Daisy's dock. According to Jordan, Gatsby has asked her to convince Nick to arrange a reunion between Gatsby and Daisy. Because he is terrified that Daisy will refuse to see him, Gatsby wants Nick to invite Daisy to tea. Without Daisy's knowledge, Gatsby intends to come to the tea at Nick's house as well, surprising her and forcing her to see him.

ANALYSIS

Though Nick's first impression of Gatsby is of his boundless hope for the future, Chapter IV concerns itself largely with the mysterious question of Gatsby's past. Gatsby's description of his background to Nick is a daunting puzzle—though he rattles off a seemingly far-fetched account of his grand upbringing and heroic exploits, he produces what appears to be proof of his story. Nick finds Gatsby's story "threadbare" at first, but he eventually accepts at least part of it when he sees the photograph and the medal. He realizes Gatsby's peculiarity, however. In calling him a "character," he highlights Gatsby's strange role as an actor.

The luncheon with Wolfshiem gives Nick his first unpleasant impression that Gatsby's fortune may not have been obtained honestly. Nick perceives that if Gatsby has connections with such shady characters as Wolfshiem, he might be involved in organized crime or bootlegging. It is important to remember the setting of *The Great Gatsby,* in terms of both the symbolic role of the novel's physical locations and the book's larger attempt to capture the essence of America in the mid-1920s. The pervasiveness of bootlegging and organized crime, combined with the burgeoning stock market and vast increase in the wealth of the general public during this era, contributed largely to the heedless, excessive pleasure-seeking and sense of abandon that permeate *The Great Gatsby*. For Gatsby, who throws the most sumptuous parties of all and who seems richer than anyone else, to have ties to the world of bootleg alcohol would only make him a more perfect symbol of the strange combination of moral decadence and vibrant optimism that Fitzgerald portrays as the spirit of 1920s America.

On the other hand, Jordan's story paints Gatsby as a lovesick, innocent young soldier, desperately trying to win the woman of his dreams. Now that Gatsby is a full-fledged character in the novel, the bizarre inner conflict that enables Nick to feel such contradictory admiration and repulsion for him becomes fully apparent—whereas Gatsby the lovesick soldier is an attractive figure, representative of hope and authenticity, Gatsby the crooked businessman, representative of greed and moral corruption, is not.

As well as shedding light on Gatsby's past, Chapter IV illuminates a matter of great personal meaning for Gatsby: the object of his hope, the green light toward which he reaches. Gatsby's love for Daisy is the source of his romantic hopefulness and the meaning of his yearning for the green light in Chapter I. That light, so mysterious in the first chapter, becomes the symbol of Gatsby's dream, his love for Daisy, and his attempt to make that love real. The green light is one of the most important symbols in *The Great Gatsby*. Like the eyes of Doctor T. J. Eckleburg, the green light can be interpreted in many ways, and Fitzgerald leaves the precise meaning of the symbol to the reader's interpretation. Many critics have suggested that, in addition to representing Gatsby's love for Daisy, the green light represents the American dream itself. Gatsby's irresistible longing to achieve his dream, the connection of his dream to the pursuit of money and material success, the boundless optimism with which he goes about achieving his dream, and the sense of his having created a new identity in a new place all reflect the coarse combination of pioneer individualism and uninhibited materialism that Fitzgerald perceived as dominating 1920s American life.

CHAPTER V

SUMMARY

That night, Nick comes home from the city after a date with Jordan. He is surprised to see Gatsby's mansion lit up brightly, but it seems to be unoccupied, as the house is totally silent. As Nick walks home, Gatsby startles him by approaching him from across the lawn. Gatsby seems agitated and almost desperate to make Nick happy—he invites him to Coney Island, then for a swim in his pool. Nick realizes that Gatsby is nervous because he wants Nick to agree to his plan of inviting Daisy over for tea. Nick tells Gatsby that he will help him with the plan. Overjoyed, Gatsby immediately offers to have someone cut Nick's grass. He also offers him the chance to make some money by joining him in some business he does on the side—business that does not involve Meyer Wolfshiem. Nick is slightly offended that Gatsby wants to pay him for arranging the meeting with Daisy and refuses Gatsby's offers, but he still agrees to call Daisy and invite her to his house.

It rains on the day of the meeting, and Gatsby becomes terribly nervous. Despite the rain, Gatsby sends a gardener over to cut Nick's grass and sends another man over with flowers. Gatsby worries that even if Daisy accepts his advances, things between them will not be the same as they were in Louisville. Daisy arrives, but when Nick brings her into the house, he finds that Gatsby has suddenly disappeared. There is a knock at the door. Gatsby enters, having returned from a walk around the house in the rain.

At first, Gatsby's reunion with Daisy is terribly awkward. Gatsby knocks Nick's clock over and tells Nick sorrowfully that the meeting was a mistake. After he leaves the two alone for half an hour, however, Nick returns to find them radiantly happy—Daisy shedding tears of joy and Gatsby glowing. Outside, the rain has stopped, and Gatsby invites Nick and Daisy over to his house, where he shows them his possessions. Daisy is overwhelmed by his luxurious lifestyle, and when he shows her his extensive collection of English shirts, she begins to cry. Gatsby tells Daisy about his long nights spent outside, staring at the green light at the end of her dock, dreaming about their future happiness.

Nick wonders whether Daisy can possibly live up to Gatsby's vision of her. Gatsby seems to have idealized Daisy in his mind to the extent that the real Daisy, charming as she is, will almost certainly fail to live up to his expectations. For the moment, however, their romance seems fully rekindled. Gatsby calls in Klipspringer, a strange character who seems to live at Gatsby's mansion, and has him play the piano. Klipspringer plays a popular song called "Ain't We Got Fun?" Nick quickly realizes that Gatsby and Daisy have forgotten that he is there. Quietly, Nick gets up and leaves Gatsby and Daisy alone together.

ANALYSIS

Chapter V is the pivotal chapter of *The Great Gatsby*, as Gatsby's reunion with Daisy is the hinge on which the novel swings. Before this event, the story of their relationship exists only in prospect, as Gatsby moves toward a dream that no one else can discern. Afterward, the plot shifts its focus to the romance between Gatsby and Daisy, and the tensions in their relationship actualize themselves. After Gatsby's history with Daisy is revealed, a meeting between the two becomes inevitable, and it is highly appropriate that the theme of the past's significance to the future is evoked in this chapter. As the novel explores ideas of love, excess, and the American dream, it becomes clearer and clearer to the reader that Gatsby's emotional frame is out of sync with the passage of time. His nervousness about the present and about how Daisy's attitude toward him may have changed causes him to knock over Nick's clock, symbolizing the clumsiness of his attempt to stop time and retrieve the past.

Gatsby's character throughout his meeting with Daisy is at its purest and most revealing. The theatrical quality that he often projects falls away, and for once all of his responses seem genuine. He forgets to play the role of the Oxford-educated socialite and shows himself to be a love-struck, awkward young man. Daisy, too, is moved to sincerity when her emotions get the better of her. Before the meeting, Daisy displays her usual sardonic humor; when Nick invites her to tea and asks her not to bring Tom, she responds, "Who is 'Tom'?" Yet, seeing Gatsby strips her of her glib veneer. When she goes to Gatsby's house, she is overwhelmed by honest tears of joy at his success and sobs upon seeing his piles of expensive English shirts.

One of the main qualities that Nick claims to possess, along with honesty, is tolerance. On one level, his arrangement of the meeting brings his practice of tolerance almost to the level of complicity—just as he tolerantly observes Tom's merrymaking with Myrtle, so he facilitates the commencement of an extramarital affair for Daisy, potentially helping to wreck her marriage. Ironically, all the while Nick is disgusted by the moral decay that he witnesses among the rich in New York. However, Nick's actions may be at least partially justified by the intense and sincere love that Gatsby and Daisy clearly feel for each other, a love that Nick perceives to be absent from Daisy's relationship with Tom.

In this chapter, Gatsby's house is compared several times to that of a feudal lord, and his imported clothes, antiques, and luxuries all display a nostalgia for the lifestyle of a British aristocrat. Though

Nick and Daisy are amazed and dazzled by Gatsby's splendid possessions, a number of things in Nick's narrative suggest that something
is not right about this transplantation of an aristocrat's lifestyle into
democratic America. For example, Nick notes that the brewer who
built the house in which Gatsby now lives tried to pay the neighbor-
ing villagers to have their roofs thatched, to complement the style
of the mansion. They refused, Nick says, because Americans are
obstinately unwilling to play the role of peasants. Thomas Jeffer-
son and the other founding fathers envisioned America as a place
that would be free of the injustices of class and caste, a place where
people from humble backgrounds would be free to try to improve
themselves economically and socially. Chapter V suggests that this
dream of improvement, carried to its logical conclusion, results in a
superficial imitation of the old European social system that America
left behind.

CHAPTER VI

SUMMARY

*The truth was that Jay Gatsby, of West Egg, Long
Island, sprang from his Platonic conception of himself.*
(See QUOTATIONS, *p. 43*)

The rumors about Gatsby continue to circulate in New York—a
reporter even travels to Gatsby's mansion hoping to interview him.
Having learned the truth about Gatsby's early life sometime before
writing his account, Nick now interrupts the story to relate Gatsby's
personal history—not as it is rumored to have occurred, nor as
Gatsby claimed it occurred, but as it really happened.

Gatsby was born James Gatz on a North Dakota farm, and
though he attended college at St. Olaf's in Minnesota, he dropped
out after two weeks, loathing the humiliating janitorial work by
means of which he paid his tuition. He worked on Lake Superior
the next summer fishing for salmon and digging for clams. One day,
he saw a yacht owned by Dan Cody, a wealthy copper mogul, and
rowed out to warn him about an impending storm. The grateful
Cody took young Gatz, who gave his name as Jay Gatsby, on board
his yacht as his personal assistant. Traveling with Cody to the Bar-
bary Coast and the West Indies, Gatsby fell in love with wealth and
luxury. Cody was a heavy drinker, and one of Gatsby's jobs was
to look after him during his drunken binges. This gave Gatsby a

healthy respect for the dangers of alcohol and convinced him not to become a drinker himself. When Cody died, he left Gatsby $25,000, but Cody's mistress prevented him from claiming his inheritance. Gatsby then dedicated himself to becoming a wealthy and successful man.

Nick sees neither Gatsby nor Daisy for several weeks after their reunion at Nick's house. Stopping by Gatsby's house one afternoon, he is alarmed to find Tom Buchanan there. Tom has stopped for a drink at Gatsby's house with Mr. and Mrs. Sloane, with whom he has been out riding. Gatsby seems nervous and agitated, and tells Tom awkwardly that he knows Daisy. Gatsby invites Tom and the Sloanes to stay for dinner, but they refuse. To be polite, they invite Gatsby to dine with them, and he accepts, not realizing the insincerity of the invitation. Tom is contemptuous of Gatsby's lack of social grace and highly critical of Daisy's habit of visiting Gatsby's house alone. He is suspicious, but he has not yet discovered Gatsby and Daisy's love.

The following Saturday night, Tom and Daisy go to a party at Gatsby's house. Though Tom has no interest in the party, his dislike for Gatsby causes him to want to keep an eye on Daisy. Gatsby's party strikes Nick much more unfavorably this time around—he finds the revelry oppressive and notices that even Daisy has a bad time. Tom upsets her by telling her that Gatsby's fortune comes from bootlegging. She angrily replies that Gatsby's wealth comes from a chain of drugstores that he owns.

Gatsby seeks out Nick after Tom and Daisy leave the party; he is unhappy because Daisy has had such an unpleasant time. Gatsby wants things to be exactly the same as they were before he left Louisville: he wants Daisy to leave Tom so that he can be with her. Nick reminds Gatsby that he cannot re-create the past. Gatsby, distraught, protests that he can. He believes that his money can accomplish anything as far as Daisy is concerned. As he walks amid the debris from the party, Nick thinks about the first time Gatsby kissed Daisy, the moment when his dream of Daisy became the dominant force in his life. Now that he has her, Nick reflects, his dream is effectively over.

ANALYSIS

Chapter VI further explores the topic of social class as it relates to Gatsby. Nick's description of Gatsby's early life reveals the sensitivity to status that spurs Gatsby on. His humiliation at having to work as a janitor in college contrasts with the promise that he experiences when he meets Dan Cody, who represents the attainment of everything that

Gatsby wants. Acutely aware of his poverty, the young Gatsby develops a powerful obsession with amassing wealth and status. Gatsby's act of rechristening himself symbolizes his desire to jettison his lower-class identity and recast himself as the wealthy man he envisions.

It is easy to see how a man who has gone to such great lengths to achieve wealth and luxury would find Daisy so alluring: for her, the aura of wealth and luxury comes effortlessly. She is able to take her position for granted, and she becomes, for Gatsby, the epitome of everything that he invented "Jay Gatsby" to achieve. As is true throughout the book, Gatsby's power to make his dreams real is what makes him "great." In this chapter, it becomes clear that his most powerfully realized dream is his own identity, his sense of self. It is important to realize, in addition, that Gatsby's conception of Daisy is itself a dream. He thinks of her as the sweet girl who loved him in Louisville, blinding himself to the reality that she would never desert her own class and background to be with him. ·

Fitzgerald continues to explore the theme of social class by illustrating the contempt with which the aristocratic East Eggers, Tom and the Sloanes, regard Gatsby. Even though Gatsby seems to have as much money as they do, he lacks their sense of social nuance and easy, aristocratic grace. As a result, they mock and despise him for being "new money." As the division between East Egg and West Egg shows, even among the very rich there are class distinctions.

It is worth noting that Fitzgerald never shows the reader a single scene from Gatsby's affair with Daisy. The narrative is Nick's story, and, aside from when they remake each other's acquaintance, Nick never sees Gatsby and Daisy alone together. Perhaps Nick's friendship with Gatsby allows him to empathize with his pain at not having Daisy, and that Nick refrains from depicting their affair out of a desire not to malign him. Whatever the reason, Fitzgerald leaves the details of their affair to the reader's imagination, and instead exposes the menacing suspicion and mistrust on Tom's part that will eventually lead to a confrontation.

CHAPTER VII

SUMMARY

Preoccupied by his love for Daisy, Gatsby calls off his parties, which were primarily a means to lure Daisy. He also fires his servants to prevent gossip and replaces them with shady individuals connected to Meyer Wolfshiem.

On the hottest day of the summer, Nick drives to East Egg for lunch at the house of Tom and Daisy. He finds Gatsby and Jordan Baker there as well. When the nurse brings in Daisy's baby girl, Gatsby is stunned and can hardly believe that the child is real. For her part, Daisy seems almost uninterested in her child. During the awkward afternoon, Gatsby and Daisy cannot hide their love for one another. Complaining of her boredom, Daisy asks Gatsby if he wants to go into the city. Gatsby stares at her passionately, and Tom becomes certain of their feelings for each other.

Itching for a confrontation, Tom seizes upon Daisy's suggestion that they should all go to New York together. Nick rides with Jordan and Tom in Gatsby's car, and Gatsby and Daisy ride together in Tom's car. Stopping for gas at Wilson's garage, Nick, Tom, and Jordan learn that Wilson has discovered his wife's infidelity—though not the identity of her lover—and plans to move her to the West. Under the brooding eyes of Doctor T. J. Eckleburg, Nick perceives that Tom and Wilson are in the same position.

In the oppressive New York City heat, the group decides to take a suite at the Plaza Hotel. Tom initiates his planned confrontation with Gatsby by mocking his habit of calling people "old sport." He accuses Gatsby of lying about having attended Oxford. Gatsby responds that he did attend Oxford—for five months, in an army program following the war. Tom asks Gatsby about his intentions for Daisy, and Gatsby replies that Daisy loves him, not Tom. Tom claims that he and Daisy have a history that Gatsby could not possibly understand. He then accuses Gatsby of running a bootlegging operation. Daisy, in love with Gatsby earlier in the afternoon, feels herself moving closer and closer to Tom as she observes the quarrel. Realizing he has bested Gatsby, Tom sends Daisy back to Long Island with Gatsby to prove Gatsby's inability to hurt him. As the row quiets down, Nick realizes that it is his thirtieth birthday.

Driving back to Long Island, Nick, Tom, and Jordan discover a frightening scene on the border of the valley of ashes. Someone has been fatally hit by an automobile. Michaelis, a Greek man who runs the restaurant next to Wilson's garage, tells them that Myrtle was the victim—a car coming from New York City struck her, paused, then sped away. Nick realizes that Myrtle must have been hit by Gatsby and Daisy, driving back from the city in Gatsby's big yellow automobile. Tom thinks that Wilson will remember the yellow car from that afternoon. He also assumes that Gatsby was the driver.

Back at Tom's house, Nick waits outside and finds Gatsby hiding in the bushes. Gatsby says that he has been waiting there in order to make sure that Tom did not hurt Daisy. He tells Nick that Daisy was driving when the car struck Myrtle, but that he himself will take the blame. Still worried about Daisy, Gatsby sends Nick to check on her. Nick finds Tom and Daisy eating cold fried chicken and talking. They have reconciled their differences, and Nick leaves Gatsby standing alone in the moonlight.

ANALYSIS

Chapter VII brings the conflict between Tom and Gatsby into the open, and their confrontation over Daisy brings to the surface troubling aspects of both characters. Throughout the previous chapters, hints have been accumulating about Gatsby's criminal activity. Research into the matter confirms Tom's suspicions, and he wields his knowledge of Gatsby's illegal activities in front of everyone to disgrace him. Likewise, Tom's sexism and hypocrisy become clearer and more obtrusive during the course of the confrontation. He has no moral qualms about his own extramarital affairs, but when faced with his wife's infidelity, he assumes the position of outraged victim.

The importance of time and the past manifests itself in the confrontation between Gatsby and Tom. Gatsby's obsession with recovering a blissful past compels him to order Daisy to tell Tom that she has never loved him. Gatsby needs to know that she has always loved him, that she has always been emotionally loyal to him. Similarly, pleading with Daisy, Tom invokes their intimate personal history to remind her that she has had feelings for him; by controlling the past, Tom eradicates Gatsby's vision of the future. That Tom feels secure enough to send Daisy back to East Egg with Gatsby confirms Nick's observation that Gatsby's dream is dead.

Gatsby's decision to take the blame for Daisy demonstrates the deep love he still feels for her and illustrates the basic nobility that defines his character. Disregarding her almost capricious lack of concern for him, Gatsby sacrifices himself for Daisy. The image of a pitiable Gatsby keeping watch outside her house while she and Tom sit comfortably within is an indelible image that both allows the reader to look past Gatsby's criminality and functions as a moving metaphor for the love Gatsby feels toward Daisy. Nick's parting from Gatsby at the end of this chapter parallels his first sighting of Gatsby at the end of Chapter I. In both cases, Gatsby stands alone in the moonlight pining for Daisy. In the earlier instance, he stretches his arms out toward the green light across the water, optimistic about the future. In this instance, he has made it past the green light, onto the lawn of Daisy's house, but his dream is gone forever.

CHAPTER VIII

SUMMARY

After the day's traumatic events, Nick passes a sleepless night. Before dawn, he rises restlessly and goes to visit Gatsby at his mansion. Gatsby tells him that he waited at Daisy's until four o'clock in the morning and that nothing happened—Tom did not try to hurt her and Daisy did not come outside. Nick suggests that Gatsby forget about Daisy and leave Long Island, but Gatsby refuses to consider leaving Daisy behind. Gatsby, melancholy, tells Nick about courting Daisy in Louisville in 1917. He says that he loved her for her youth and vitality, and idolized her social position, wealth, and popularity. He adds that she was the first girl to whom he ever felt close and that he lied about his background to make her believe that he was worthy of her. Eventually, he continues, he and Daisy made love, and he felt as though he had married her. She promised to wait for him when he left for the war, but then she married Tom, whose social position was solid and who had the approval of her parents.

Gatsby's gardener interrupts the story to tell Gatsby that he plans to drain the pool. The previous day was the hottest of the summer, but autumn is in the air this morning, and the gardener worries that falling leaves will clog the pool drains. Gatsby tells the gardener to wait a day; he has never used the pool, he says, and wants to go for a swim. Nick has stayed so long talking to Gatsby that he is very late for work. He finally says goodbye to Gatsby. As he walks away, he turns back and shouts that Gatsby is worth more than the Buchanans and all of their friends.

Nick goes to his office, but he feels too distracted to work, and even refuses to meet Jordan Baker for a date. The focus of his narrative then shifts to relate to the reader what happened at the garage after Myrtle was killed (the details of which Nick learns from Michaelis): George Wilson stays up all night talking to Michaelis about Myrtle. He tells him that before Myrtle died, he confronted her about her lover and told her that she could not hide her sin from the eyes of God. The morning after the accident, the eyes of Doctor T. J. Eckleburg, illuminated by the dawn, overwhelm Wilson. He believes they are the eyes of God and leaps to the conclusion that whoever was driving the car that killed Myrtle must have been her lover. He decides that God demands revenge and leaves to track down the owner of the car. He looks for Tom, because he knows that Tom is familiar with the car's owner—he saw Tom driving the car earlier that day but knows Tom could not have been the driver since Tom arrived after the accident in a different car with Nick and Jordan. Wilson eventually goes to Gatsby's house, where he finds Gatsby lying on an air mattress in the pool, floating in the water and looking up at the sky. Wilson shoots Gatsby, killing him instantly, then shoots himself.

Nick hurries back to West Egg and finds Gatsby floating dead in his pool. Nick imagines Gatsby's final thoughts, and pictures him disillusioned by the meaninglessness and emptiness of life without Daisy, without his dream.

ANALYSIS

Gatsby's recounting of his initial courting of Daisy provides Nick an opportunity to analyze Gatsby's love for her. Nick identifies Daisy's aura of wealth and privilege—her many clothes, perfect house, lack of fear or worry—as a central component of Gatsby's attraction to her. The reader has already seen that Gatsby idolizes both wealth and Daisy. Now it becomes clear that the two are intertwined in Gatsby's mind. Nick implicitly suggests that by making the shallow, fickle Daisy the focus of his life, Gatsby surrenders his extraordinary power of visionary hope to the simple task of amassing wealth. Gatsby's dream is reduced to a motivation for material gain because the object of his dream is unworthy of his power of dreaming, the quality that makes him "great" in the first place.

In this way, Gatsby continues to function as a symbol of America in the 1920s, which, as Fitzgerald implies throughout the novel's exploration of wealth, has become vulgar and empty as a result of subjecting its sprawling vitality to the greedy pursuit of money. Just as the American dream—the pursuit of happiness—has degenerated into a quest for mere wealth, Gatsby's powerful dream of happiness with Daisy has become the motivation for lavish excesses and criminal activities.

Although the reader is able to perceive this degradation, Gatsby is not. For him, losing Daisy is like losing his entire world. He has longed to re-create his past with her and is now forced to talk to Nick about it in a desperate attempt to keep it alive. Even after the confrontation with Tom, Gatsby is unable to accept that his dream is dead. Though Nick implicitly understands that Daisy is not going to leave Tom for Gatsby under any circumstance, Gatsby continues to insist that she will call him.

Throughout this chapter, the narrative implicitly establishes a connection between the weather and the emotional atmosphere of the story. Just as the geographical settings of the book correspond to particular characters and themes, the weather corresponds to the plot. In the previous chapter, Gatsby's tension-filled confrontation with Tom took place on the hottest day of the summer, beneath a fiery and intense sun. Now that the fire has gone out of Gatsby's life with Daisy's decision to remain with Tom, the weather suddenly cools, and autumn creeps into the air—the gardener even wants to drain the pool to keep falling leaves from clogging the drains. In the same way that he clings to the hope of making Daisy love him the way she used to, he insists on swimming in the pool as though it were still summer. Both his downfall in Chapter VII and his death in Chapter VIII result from his stark refusal to accept what he cannot control: the passage of time.

Gatsby has made Daisy a symbol of everything he values, and made the green light on her dock a symbol of his destiny with her. Thinking about Gatsby's death, Nick suggests that all symbols are created by the mind—they do not possess any inherent meaning; rather, people invest them with meaning. Nick writes that Gatsby must have realized "what a grotesque thing a rose is." The rose has been a conventional symbol of beauty throughout centuries of poetry. Nick suggests that roses aren't inherently beautiful, and that people only view them that way because they choose to do so. Daisy is "grotesque" in the same way: Gatsby has invested her with beauty and meaning by making her the object of his dream. Had Gatsby not imbued her with such value, Daisy would be simply an idle, bored, rich young woman with no particular moral strength or loyalty.

Likewise, though they suggest divine scrutiny both to the reader and to Wilson, the eyes of Doctor T. J. Eckleburg are disturbing in part because they are not the eyes of God. They have no precise, fixed meaning. George Wilson takes Doctor T. J. Eckleburg's eyes for the all-seeing eyes of God and derives his misguided belief that Myrtle's killer must have been her lover from that inference. George's assertion that the eyes represent a moral standard, the upholding of which means that he must avenge Myrtle's death, becomes a gross parallel to Nick's desire to find a moral center in his life. The eyes of Doctor T. J. Eckleburg can mean anything a character or reader wants them to, but they look down on a world devoid of meaning, value, and beauty—a world in which dreams are exposed as illusions, and cruel, unfeeling men such as Tom receive the love of women longed for by dreamers such as Gatsby and Wilson.

Chapter IX

Summary

Writing two years after Gatsby's death, Nick describes the events that surrounded the funeral. Swarms of reporters, journalists, and gossipmongers descend on the mansion in the aftermath of the murder. Wild, untrue stories, more exaggerated than the rumors about Gatsby when he was throwing his parties, circulate about the nature of Gatsby's relationship to Myrtle and Wilson. Feeling that Gatsby would not want to go through a funeral alone, Nick tries to hold a large funeral for him, but all of Gatsby's former friends and acquaintances have either disappeared—Tom and Daisy, for instance, move away with no forwarding address—or refuse to come, like Meyer Wolfshiem and Klipspringer. The latter claims that he has a social engagement in Westport and asks Nick to send along his tennis shoes. Outraged, Nick hangs up on him. The only people to attend the funeral are Nick, Owl Eyes, a few servants, and Gatsby's father, Henry C. Gatz, who has come all the way from Minnesota. Henry Gatz is proud of his son and saves a picture of his house. He also fills Nick in on Gatsby's early life, showing him a book in which a young Gatsby had written a schedule for self-improvement.

Sick of the East and its empty values, Nick decides to move back to the Midwest. He breaks off his relationship with Jordan, who suddenly claims that she has become engaged to another man. Just before he leaves, Nick encounters Tom on Fifth Avenue in New York City. Nick initially refuses to shake Tom's hand but eventually accepts. Tom tells him that he was the one who told Wilson that Gatsby owned the car that killed Myrtle, and describes how greatly he suffered when he had to give up the apartment he kept in the city for his affair. He says that Gatsby deserved to die. Nick comes to the conclusion that Tom and Daisy are careless and uncaring people and that they destroy people and things, knowing that their money will shield them from ever having to face any negative consequences.

Nick muses that, in some ways, this story is a story of the West even though it has taken place entirely on the East Coast. Nick, Jordan, Tom, and Daisy are all from west of the Appalachians, and Nick believes that the reactions of each, himself included, to living the fast-paced, lurid lifestyle of the East has shaped his or her behavior. Nick remembers life in the Midwest, full of snow, trains, and Christmas wreaths, and thinks that the East seems grotesque and distorted by comparison.

On his last night in West Egg before moving back to Minnesota, Nick walks over to Gatsby's empty mansion and erases an obscene word that someone has written on the steps. He sprawls out on the beach behind Gatsby's house and looks up. As the moon rises, he imagines the island with no houses and considers what it must have looked like to the explorers who discovered the New World centuries before. He imagines that America was once a goal for dreamers and explorers, just as Daisy was for Gatsby. He pictures the green land of America as the green light shining from Daisy's dock, and muses that Gatsby—whose wealth and success so closely echo the American dream—failed to realize that the dream had already ended, that his goals had become hollow and empty. Nick senses that people everywhere are motivated by similar dreams and by a desire to move forward into a future in which their dreams are realized. Nick envisions their struggles to create that future as boats moving in a body of water against a current that inevitably carries them back into the past.

> I see now that this has been a story of the West, after all—Tom and Gatsby, Daisy and Jordan and I, were all Westerners, and perhaps we possessed some deficiency in common which made us subtly unadaptable to Eastern life.
>
> (See QUOTATIONS, p. 44)

ANALYSIS

Nick thinks of America not just as a nation but as a geographical entity, land with distinct regions embodying contrasting sets of values. The Midwest, he thinks, seems dreary and pedestrian compared to the excitement of the East, but the East is merely a glittering surface—it lacks the moral center of the Midwest. This fundamental moral depravity dooms the characters of *The Great Gatsby*—all Westerners, as Nick observes—to failure. The "quality of distortion" that lures them to the East disgusts Nick and contributes to his decision to move back to Minnesota.

There is another significance to the fact that all of the major characters are Westerners, however. Throughout American history, the West has been seen as a land of promise and possibility—the very emblem of American ideals. Tom and Daisy, like other members of the upper class, have betrayed America's democratic ideals by perpetuating a rigid class structure that excludes newcomers from its upper reaches, much like the feudal aristocracy that America had left behind. Gatsby, alone among Nick's acquaintances, has the audacity and nobility of spirit to dream of creating a radically different future for himself, but his dream ends in failure for several reasons: his methods are criminal, he can never gain acceptance into the American aristocracy (which he would have to do to win Daisy), and his new identity is largely an act. It is not at all clear what Gatsby's failure says about the dreams and aspirations of Americans generally, but Fitzgerald's novel certainly questions the idea of an America in which all things are possible if one simply tries hard enough.

The problem of American dreams is closely related to the problem of how to deal with the past. America was founded through a dramatic declaration of independence from its own past—its European roots—and it promises its citizens the potential for unlimited advancement, regardless of where they come from or how poor their backgrounds are. Gatsby's failure suggests that it may be impossible for one to disown one's past so completely. There seems to be an impossible divide separating Gatsby and Daisy, which is certainly part of her allure for him. This divide clearly comes from their different backgrounds and social contexts.

Throughout the novel, Nick's judgments of the other characters are based in the values that he inherited from his father, the moral "privileges" that he refers to in the opening pages. Nick's values, so strongly rooted in the past, give him the ability to make sense out of everything in the novel except for Gatsby. In Nick's eyes, Gatsby embodies an ability to dream and to escape the past that may ultimately be impossible, but that Nick cherishes and values nonetheless. *The Great Gatsby* represents Nick's struggle to integrate his own sense of the importance of the past with the freedom from the past envisioned by Gatsby.

IMPORTANT QUOTATIONS EXPLAINED

1. I hope she'll be a fool—that's the best thing a girl can be in this world, a beautiful little fool.

Daisy speaks these words in Chapter I as she describes to Nick and Jordan her hopes for her infant daughter. While not directly relevant to the novel's main themes, this quote offers a revealing glimpse into Daisy's character. Daisy is not a fool herself but is the product of a social environment that, to a great extent, does not value intelligence in women. The older generation values subservience and docility in females, and the younger generation values thoughtless giddiness and pleasure-seeking. Daisy's remark is somewhat sardonic: while she refers to the social values of her era, she does not seem to challenge them. Instead, she describes her own boredom with life and seems to imply that a girl can have more fun if she is beautiful and simplistic. Daisy herself often tries to act such a part. She conforms to the social standard of American femininity in the 1920s in order to avoid such tension-filled issues as her undying love for Gatsby.

2. He had one of those rare smiles with a quality of eternal reassurance in it, that you may come across four or five times in life. It faced, or seemed to face, the whole external world for an instant and then concentrated on you with an irresistible prejudice in your favor. It understood you just as far as you wanted to be understood, believed in you as you would like to believe in yourself.

This passage occurs in Chapter III as part of Nick's first close examination of Gatsby's character and appearance. This description of Gatsby's smile captures both the theatrical quality of Gatsby's character and his charisma. Additionally, it encapsulates the manner in which Gatsby appears to the outside world, an image Fitzgerald slowly deconstructs as the novel progresses toward Gatsby's death in Chapter VIII. One of the main facets of Gatsby's persona is that he acts out a role that he defined for himself when he was seventeen years old. His smile seems to be both an important part of the role and a result of the singular combination of hope and imagination that enables him to play it so effectively. Here, Nick describes Gatsby's rare focus—he has the ability to make anyone he smiles at feel as though he has chosen that person out of "the whole external world," reflecting that person's most optimistic conception of him- or herself.

QUOTATIONS

3. The truth was that Jay Gatsby, of West Egg, Long Island, sprang from his Platonic conception of himself. He was a son of God—a phrase which, if it means anything, means just that—and he must be about His Father's business, the service of a vast, vulgar, and meretricious beauty. So he invented just the sort of Jay Gatsby that a seventeen year old boy would be likely to invent, and to this conception he was faithful to the end.

In Chapter VI, when Nick finally describes Gatsby's early history, he uses this striking comparison between Gatsby and Jesus Christ to illuminate Gatsby's creation of his own identity. Fitzgerald was probably influenced in drawing this parallel by a nineteenth-century book by Ernest Renan entitled *The Life of Jesus*. This book presents Jesus as a figure who essentially decided to make himself the son of God, then brought himself to ruin by refusing to recognize the reality that denied his self-conception. Renan describes a Jesus who is "faithful to his self-created dream but scornful of the factual truth that finally crushes him and his dream"—a very appropriate description of Gatsby. Fitzgerald is known to have admired Renan's work and seems to have drawn upon it in devising this metaphor. Though the parallel between Gatsby and Jesus is not an important motif in *The Great Gatsby*, it is nonetheless a suggestive comparison, as Gatsby transforms himself into the ideal that he envisioned for himself (a "Platonic conception of himself") as a youngster and remains committed to that ideal, despite the obstacles that society presents to the fulfillment of his dream.

4.   That's my Middle West . . . the street lamps and sleigh bells
     in the frosty dark. . . . I see now that this has been a story
     of the West, after all—Tom and Gatsby, Daisy and Jordan
     and I, were all Westerners, and perhaps we possessed some
     deficiency in common which made us subtly unadaptable
     to Eastern life.

This important quote from Nick's lengthy meditation in Chapter IX
brings the motif of geography in *The Great Gatsby* to a conclusion.
Throughout the novel, places are associated with themes, characters, and ideas. The East is associated with a fast-paced lifestyle,
decadent parties, crumbling moral values, and the pursuit of wealth,
while the West and the Midwest are associated with more traditional moral values. In this moment, Nick realizes for the first time
that though his story is set on the East Coast, the western character
of his acquaintances ("some deficiency in common") is the source
of the story's tensions and attitudes. He considers each character's
behavior and value choices as a reaction to the wealth-obsessed
culture of New York. This perspective contributes powerfully to
Nick's decision to leave the East Coast and return to Minnesota, as
the infeasibility of Nick's Midwestern values in New York society
mirrors the impracticality of Gatsby's dream.

5.   Gatsby believed in the green light, the orgastic future that
     year by year recedes before us. It eluded us then, but that's
     no matter—tomorrow we will run faster, stretch out our
     arms farther. . . . And then one fine morning—
        So we beat on, boats against the current, borne back
     ceaselessly into the past.

These words conclude the novel and find Nick returning to the
theme of the significance of the past to dreams of the future, here
represented by the green light. He focuses on the struggle of human
beings to achieve their goals by both transcending and re-creating
the past. Yet humans prove themselves unable to move beyond the
past: in the metaphoric language used here, the current draws them
backward as they row forward toward the green light. This past
functions as the source of their ideas about the future (epitomized
by Gatsby's desire to re-create 1917 in his affair with Daisy) and
they cannot escape it as they continue to struggle to transform their
dreams into reality. While they never lose their optimism ("tomor-
row we will run faster, stretch out our arms farther . . ."), they ex-
pend all of their energy in pursuit of a goal that moves ever farther
away. This apt metaphor characterizes both Gatsby's struggle and
the American dream itself. Nick's words register neither blind approval nor cynical disillusionment but rather the respectful melancholy that he ultimately brings to his study of Gatsby's life.

QUOTATIONS

KEY FACTS

FULL TITLE
The Great Gatsby

AUTHOR
F. Scott Fitzgerald

TYPE OF WORK
Novel

GENRE
Modernist novel, Jazz Age novel, novel of manners

LANGUAGE
English

TIME AND PLACE WRITTEN
1923–1924, America and France

DATE OF FIRST PUBLICATION
1925

PUBLISHER
Charles Scribner's Sons

NARRATOR
Nick Carraway; Carraway not only narrates the story but implies that he is the book's author

POINT OF VIEW
Nick Carraway narrates in both first and third person, presenting only what he himself observes. Nick alternates sections where he presents events objectively, as they appeared to him at the time, with sections where he gives his own interpretations of the story's meaning and of the motivations of the other characters.

TONE
Nick's attitudes toward Gatsby and Gatsby's story are ambivalent and contradictory. At times he seems to disapprove of Gatsby's excesses and breaches of manners and ethics, but he also romanticizes and admires Gatsby, describing the events of the novel in a nostalgic and elegiac tone.

TENSE
  Past

SETTING (TIME)
  Summer 1922

SETTINGS (PLACE)
  Long Island and New York City

PROTAGONIST
  Gatsby and/or Nick

MAJOR CONFLICT
  Gatsby has amassed a vast fortune in order to win the affections
  of the upper-class Daisy Buchanan, but his mysterious past
  stands in the way of his being accepted by her.

RISING ACTION
  Gatsby's lavish parties, Gatsby's arrangement of a meeting with
  Daisy at Nick's

CLIMAX
  There are two possible climaxes: Gatsby's reunion with Daisy in
  Chapters V–VI; the confrontation between Gatsby and Tom in
  the Plaza Hotel in Chapter VII.

FALLING ACTION
  Daisy's rejection of Gatsby, Myrtle's death, Gatsby's murder

THEMES
  The decline of the American dream, the spirit of the 1920s,
  the difference between social classes, the role of symbols in the
  human conception of meaning, the role of the past in dreams of
  the future

MOTIFS
  The connection between events and weather, the connection
  between geographical location and social values, images of
  time, extravagant parties, the quest for wealth

SYMBOLS
  The green light on Daisy's dock, the eyes of Doctor T. J.
  Eckleburg, the valley of ashes, Gatsby's parties, East Egg,
  West Egg

KEY FACTS

FORESHADOWING

The car wreck after Gatsby's party in Chapter III, Owl Eyes's comments about the theatricality of Gatsby's life, the mysterious telephone calls Gatsby receives from Chicago and Philadelphia

STUDY QUESTIONS

1. *Discuss Gatsby's character as Nick perceives him throughout the novel. What makes Gatsby "great"?*

In one sense, the title of the novel is ironic; the title character is neither "great" nor named Gatsby. He is a criminal whose real name is James Gatz, and the life he has created for himself is an illusion. By the same token, the title of the novel refers to the theatrical skill with which Gatsby makes this illusion seem real: the moniker "*the Great Gatsby*" suggests the sort of vaudeville billing that would have been given to an acrobat, an escape artist, or a magician.

Nick is particularly taken with Gatsby and considers him a great figure. He sees both the extraordinary quality of hope that Gatsby possesses and his idealistic dream of loving Daisy in a perfect world. Though Nick recognizes Gatsby's flaws the first time he meets him, he cannot help but admire Gatsby's brilliant smile, his romantic idealization of Daisy, and his yearning for the future. The private Gatsby who stretches his arms out toward the green light on Daisy's dock seems somehow more real than the vulgar, social Gatsby who wears a pink suit to his party and calls everyone "old sport." Nick alone among the novel's characters recognizes that Gatsby's love for Daisy has less to do with Daisy's inner qualities than with Gatsby's own. That is, Gatsby makes Daisy his dream because his heart demands a dream, not because Daisy truly deserves the passion that Gatsby feels for her. Further, Gatsby impresses Nick with his power to make his dreams come true—as a child he dreamed of wealth and luxury, and he has attained them, albeit through criminal means. As a man, he dreams of Daisy, and for a while he wins her, too. In a world without a moral center, in which attempting to fulfill one's dreams is like rowing a boat against the current, Gatsby's power to dream lifts him above the meaningless and amoral pleasure-seeking of New York society. In Nick's view, Gatsby's capacity to dream makes him "great" despite his flaws and eventual undoing.

2.   *What is Nick like as a narrator? Is he a reliable*
     storyteller, or does his version of events seem
     suspect? How do his qualities as a character affect his
     narration?

Nick's description of himself in the opening chapter holds true throughout the novel: he is tolerant and slow to judge, someone with whom people feel comfortable sharing their secrets. His willingness to describe himself and the contours of his thoughts even when they are inconsistent or incomplete—his conflicted feelings about Gatsby, for instance, or the long musing at the end of the novel—makes him seem trustworthy and thoughtful. His position in relation to the other characters gives him a perfect vantage point from which to tell the story—he is Daisy's cousin, Tom's old college friend, and Gatsby's neighbor, and all three trust and rely on him. Though Nick participates in this story and its events certainly affect him, *The Great Gatsby* is not really his story in the sense of being about him. However, it is his story in the sense that it is of crucial importance to him: he defines himself in the process of writing it. Indeed, he struggles with the story's meaning even as he tells it. Though Nick professes to admire Gatsby's passion as a lover and a dreamer, Nick's own actions in his relationship with Jordan Baker cast an ironic pall over his admiration: with Jordan, Nick is guarded, cautious, and skeptical. Overall, Nick suggests that Gatsby is an exception to his usual ways of understanding and judging the world, and that his attraction to Gatsby creates a conflict within himself.

STUDY QUESTIONS

3. *What are some of* THE GREAT GATSBY's *most
important symbols? What does the novel have to say
about the role of symbols in life?*

Apart from geographic locations, the two most important symbols
in the novel are the green light at the end of Daisy's dock and the
eyes of Doctor T. J. Eckleburg. The first is a perfect example of the
manner in which characters in *The Great Gatsby* infuse symbols
with meaning—the green light is only a green light, but to Gatsby it
becomes the embodiment of his dream for the future, and it beckons
to him in the night like a vision of the fulfillment of his desires. The
eyes of Doctor T. J. Eckleburg work in the same fashion, although
their meaning is less fixed. Until George Wilson decides that they
are the eyes of God, representing a moral imperative on which he
must act, the eyes are simply an unsettling, unexplained image, as
they stare down over the valley of ashes. The eyes of Doctor T. J.
Eckleburg thus emphasize the lack of a fixed relationship between
symbols and what they symbolize: the eyes could mean anything
to any observer, but they tend to make observers feel as though
they are the ones being scrutinized. They seem to stare down at the
world blankly, without the need for meaning that drives the human
characters of the novel.

In general, symbols in the novel are intimately connected to
dreams: Gatsby's dream of Daisy causes him to associate her image
with everything he values, just as he associates the green light with his
dream for the future. In reading and interpreting *The Great Gatsby,*
it is at least as important to consider how characters think about
symbols as it is to consider the qualities of the symbols themselves.

4. *How does the geography of the novel dictate its themes and characters? What role does setting play in* THE GREAT GATSBY?

Each of the four important geographical locations in the novel—West Egg, East Egg, the valley of ashes, and New York City—corresponds to a particular theme or type of character encountered in the story. West Egg is like Gatsby, full of garish extravagance, symbolizing the emergence of the new rich alongside the established aristocracy of the 1920s. East Egg is like the Buchanans, wealthy, possessing high social status, and powerful, symbolizing the old upper class that continued to dominate the American social landscape. The valley of ashes is like George Wilson, desolate, desperate, and utterly without hope, symbolizing the moral decay of American society hidden by the glittering surface of upper-class extravagance. New York City is simply chaos, an abundant swell of variety and life, associated with the "quality of distortion" that Nick perceives in the East.

Setting is extremely important to *The Great Gatsby*, as it reinforces the themes and character traits that drive the novel's critical events. Even the weather matches the flow of the plot. Gatsby's reunion with Daisy begins in a ferocious thunderstorm and reaches its happiest moment just as the sun comes out. Tom's confrontation with Gatsby occurs on the hottest day of the summer. Finally, Gatsby's death occurs just as autumn creeps into the air. The specificity of the settings in *The Great Gatsby* contributes greatly to the creation of distinct zones in which the conflicting values of various characters are forced to confront each other.

How to Write
Literary Analysis

The Literary Essay: A Step-by-Step Guide

When you read for pleasure, your only goal is enjoyment. You might find yourself reading to get caught up in an exciting story, to learn about an interesting time or place, or just to pass time. Maybe you're looking for inspiration, guidance, or a reflection of your own life. There are as many different, valid ways of reading a book as there are books in the world.

When you read a work of literature in an English class, however, you're being asked to read in a special way: you're being asked to perform *literary analysis*. To analyze something means to break it down into smaller parts and then examine how those parts work, both individually and together. Literary analysis involves examining all the parts of a novel, play, short story, or poem—elements such as character, setting, tone, and imagery—and thinking about how the author uses those elements to create certain effects.

A literary essay isn't a book review: you're not being asked whether or not you liked a book or whether you'd recommend it to another reader. A literary essay also isn't like the kind of book report you wrote when you were younger, where your teacher wanted you to summarize the book's action. A high school- or college-level literary essay asks, "How does this piece of literature actually work?" "How does it do what it does?" and, "Why might the author have made the choices he or she did?"

The Seven Steps
No one is born knowing how to analyze literature; it's a skill you learn and a process you can master. As you gain more practice with this kind of thinking and writing, you'll be able to craft a method that works best for you. But until then, here are seven basic steps to writing a well-constructed literary essay:

1. *Ask questions*
2. *Collect evidence*
3. *Construct a thesis*

53

4. Develop and organize arguments
5. Write the introduction
6. Write the body paragraphs
7. Write the conclusion

─────────────────────

1. Ask Questions

When you're assigned a literary essay in class, your teacher will often provide you with a list of writing prompts. Lucky you! Now all you have to do is choose one. Do yourself a favor and pick a topic that interests you. You'll have a much better (not to mention easier) time if you start off with something you enjoy thinking about. If you are asked to come up with a topic by yourself, though, you might start to feel a little panicked. Maybe you have too many ideas—or none at all. Don't worry. Take a deep breath and start by asking yourself these questions:

- **What struck you?** Did a particular image, line, or scene linger in your mind for a long time? If it fascinated you, chances are you can draw on it to write a fascinating essay.

- **What confused you?** Maybe you were surprised to see a character act in a certain way, or maybe you didn't understand why the book ended the way it did. Confusing moments in a work of literature are like a loose thread in a sweater: if you pull on it, you can unravel the entire thing. Ask yourself why the author chose to write about that character or scene the way he or she did and you might tap into some important insights about the work as a whole.

- **Did you notice any patterns?** Is there a phrase that the main character uses constantly or an image that repeats throughout the book? If you can figure out how that pattern weaves through the work and what the significance of that pattern is, you've almost got your entire essay mapped out.

- **Did you notice any contradictions or ironies?** Great works of literature are complex; great literary essays recognize and explain those complexities. Maybe the title (*Happy Days*) totally disagrees with the book's subject matter (hungry orphans dying in the woods). Maybe the main character acts one way around his family and a completely different way around his friends and associates. If you can find a way to explain a work's contradictory elements, you've got the seeds of a great essay.

At this point, you don't need to know exactly what you're going to say about your topic; you just need a place to begin your exploration. You can help direct your reading and brainstorming by formulating your topic as a *question,* which you'll then try to answer in your essay. The best questions invite critical debates and discussions, not just a rehashing of the summary. Remember, you're looking for something you can *prove or argue* based on evidence you find in the text. Finally, remember to keep the scope of your question in mind: is this a topic you can adequately address within the word or page limit you've been given? Conversely, is this a topic big enough to fill the required length?

GOOD QUESTIONS

"Are Romeo and Juliet's parents responsible for the deaths of their children?"

"Why do pigs keep showing up in LORD OF THE FLIES*?"*

"Are Dr. Frankenstein and his monster alike? How?"

BAD QUESTIONS

"What happens to Scout in TO KILL A MOCKINGBIRD*?"*

"What do the other characters in JULIUS CAESAR *think about Caesar?"*

"How does Hester Prynne in THE SCARLET LETTER *remind me of my sister?"*

---

2. COLLECT EVIDENCE

Once you know what question you want to answer, it's time to scour the book for things that will help you answer the question. Don't worry if you don't know what you want to say yet—right now you're just collecting ideas and material and letting it all percolate. Keep track of passages, symbols, images, or scenes that deal with your topic. Eventually, you'll start making connections between these examples and your thesis will emerge.

Here's a brief summary of the various parts that compose each and every work of literature. These are the elements that you will analyze in your essay, and which you will offer as evidence to support your arguments. For more on the parts of literary works, see the Glossary of Literary Terms at the end of this section.

LITERARY ANALYSIS

ELEMENTS OF STORY   These are the *what*s of the work—what happens, where it happens, and to whom it happens.

- **Plot:** All of the events and actions of the work.
- **Character:** The people who act and are acted upon in a literary work. The main character of a work is known as the *protagonist*.
- **Conflict:** The central tension in the work. In most cases, the protagonist wants something, while opposing forces (antagonists) hinder the protagonist's progress.
- **Setting:** When and where the work takes place. Elements of setting include location, time period, time of day, weather, social atmosphere, and economic conditions.
- **Narrator:** The person telling the story. The narrator may straightforwardly report what happens, convey the subjective opinions and perceptions of one or more characters, or provide commentary and opinion in his or her own voice.
- **Themes:** The main idea or message of the work—usually an abstract idea about people, society, or life in general. A work may have many themes, which may be in tension with one another.

ELEMENTS OF STYLE   These are the *how*s—how the characters speak, how the story is constructed, and how language is used throughout the work.

- **Structure and organization:** How the parts of the work are assembled. Some novels are narrated in a linear, chronological fashion, while others skip around in time. Some plays follow a traditional three- or five-act structure, while others are a series of loosely connected scenes. Some authors deliberately leave gaps in their works, leaving readers to puzzle out the missing information. A work's structure and organization can tell you a lot about the kind of message it wants to convey.
- **Point of view:** The perspective from which a story is told. In *first-person point of view*, the narrator involves him or herself in the story. ("I went to the store"; "We watched in horror as the bird slammed into the window.") A first-person narrator is usually the protagonist of the work, but not always. In *third-person point of view*, the narrator does not participate

in the story. A third-person narrator may closely follow a specific character, recounting that individual character's thoughts or experiences, or it may be what we call an *omniscient* narrator. Omniscient narrators see and know all: they can witness any event in any time or place and are privy to the inner thoughts and feelings of all characters. Remember that the narrator and the author are not the same thing!

- **Diction:** Word choice. Whether a character uses dry, clinical language or flowery prose with lots of exclamation points can tell you a lot about his or her attitude and personality.

- **Syntax:** Word order and sentence construction. Syntax is a crucial part of establishing an author's narrative voice. Ernest Hemingway, for example, is known for writing in very short, straightforward sentences, while James Joyce characteristically wrote in long, incredibly complicated lines.

- **Tone:** The mood or feeling of the text. Diction and syntax often contribute to the tone of a work. A novel written in short, clipped sentences that use small, simple words might feel brusque, cold, or matter-of-fact.

- **Imagery:** Language that appeals to the senses, representing things that can be seen, smelled, heard, tasted, or touched.

- **Figurative language:** Language that is not meant to be interpreted literally. The most common types of figurative language are *metaphors* and *similes,* which compare two unlike things in order to suggest a similarity between them—for example, "All the world's a stage," or "The moon is like a ball of green cheese." (Metaphors say one thing *is* another thing; similes claim that one thing is *like* another thing.)

---

3. CONSTRUCT A THESIS

When you've examined all the evidence you've collected and know how you want to answer the question, it's time to write your thesis statement. A *thesis* is a claim about a work of literature that needs to be supported by evidence and arguments. The thesis statement is the heart of the literary essay, and the bulk of your paper will be spent trying to prove this claim. A good thesis will be:

- **Arguable**. "*The Great Gatsby* describes New York society in the 1920s" isn't a thesis—it's a fact.

- **Provable through textual evidence**. "*Hamlet* is a confusing but ultimately very well-written play" is a weak thesis because it offers the writer's personal opinion about the book. Yes, it's arguable, but it's not a claim that can be proved or supported with examples taken from the play itself.

- **Surprising**. "Both George and Lenny change a great deal in *Of Mice and Men*" is a weak thesis because it's obvious. A really strong thesis will argue for a reading of the text that is not immediately apparent.

- **Specific.** "Dr. Frankenstein's monster tells us a lot about the human condition" is *almost* a really great thesis statement, but it's still too vague. What does the writer mean by "a lot"? *How* does the monster tell us so much about the human condition?

GOOD THESIS STATEMENTS

Question: In *Romeo and Juliet*, which is more powerful in shaping the lovers' story: fate or foolishness?

Thesis: "Though Shakespeare defines Romeo and Juliet as 'star-crossed lovers' and images of stars and planets appear throughout the play, a closer examination of that celestial imagery reveals that the stars are merely witnesses to the characters' foolish activities and not the causes themselves."

Question: How does the bell jar function as a symbol in Sylvia Plath's *The Bell Jar*?

Thesis: "A bell jar is a bell-shaped glass that has three basic uses: to hold a specimen for observation, to contain gases, and to maintain a vacuum. The bell jar appears in each of these capacities in *The Bell Jar*, Plath's semi-autobiographical novel, and each appearance marks a different stage in Esther's mental breakdown."

Question: Would Piggy in *The Lord of the Flies* make a good island leader if he were given the chance?

Thesis: "Though the intelligent, rational, and innovative Piggy has the mental characteristics of a good leader, he ultimately lacks the social skills necessary to be an effective one. Golding emphasizes this point by giving Piggy a foil in the charismatic Jack, whose magnetic personality allows him to capture and wield power effectively, if not always wisely."

4. DEVELOP AND ORGANIZE ARGUMENTS

The reasons and examples that support your thesis will form the middle paragraphs of your essay. Since you can't really write your thesis statement until you know how you'll structure your argument, you'll probably end up working on steps 3 and 4 at the same time.

There's no single method of argumentation that will work in every context. One essay prompt might ask you to compare and contrast two characters, while another asks you to trace an image through a given work of literature. These questions require different kinds of answers and therefore different kinds of arguments. Below, we'll discuss three common kinds of essay prompts and some strategies for constructing a solid, well-argued case.

TYPES OF LITERARY ESSAYS

- **Compare and contrast**

    Compare and contrast the characters of Huck and Jim in THE ADVENTURES OF HUCKLEBERRY FINN.

    Chances are you've written this kind of essay before. In an academic literary context, you'll organize your arguments the same way you would in any other class. You can either go *subject by subject* or *point by point*. In the former, you'll discuss one character first and then the second. In the latter, you'll choose several traits (attitude toward life, social status, images and metaphors associated with the character) and devote a paragraph to each. You may want to use a mix of these two approaches—for example, you may want to spend a paragraph a piece broadly sketching Huck's and Jim's personalities before transitioning into a paragraph or two that describes a few key points of comparison. This can be a highly effective strategy if you want to make a counterintuitive argument—that, despite seeming to be totally different, the two objects being compared are actually similar in a very important way (or vice versa). Remember that your essay should reveal something fresh or unexpected about the text, so think beyond the obvious parallels and differences.

- **Trace**

    Choose an image—for example, birds, knives, or eyes—and trace that image throughout MACBETH.

    Sounds pretty easy, right? All you need to do is read the play, underline every appearance of a knife in *Macbeth*, and then list them in your essay in the order they appear, right? Well, not exactly. Your teacher doesn't want a simple catalog of examples. He or she wants to see you make *connections* between those examples—that's the difference between summarizing and analyzing. In the *Macbeth* example above, think about the different contexts in which knives appear in the play and to what effect. In *Macbeth,* there are real knives and imagined knives; knives that kill and knives that simply threaten. Categorize and classify your examples to give them some order. Finally, always keep the overall effect in mind. After you choose and analyze your examples, you should come to some greater understanding about the work, as well as your chosen image, symbol, or phrase's role in developing the major themes and stylistic strategies of that work.

- **Debate**

  Is the society depicted in 1984 good for its citizens?

In this kind of essay, you're being asked to debate a moral, ethical, or aesthetic issue regarding the work. You might be asked to judge a character or group of characters (*Is Caesar responsible for his own demise?*) or the work itself (*Is* JANE EYRE *a feminist novel?*). For this kind of essay, there are two important points to keep in mind. First, don't simply base your arguments on your personal feelings and reactions. Every literary essay expects you to read and analyze the work, so search for evidence in the text. What do characters in *1984* have to say about the government of Oceania? What images does Orwell use that might give you a hint about his attitude toward the government? As in any debate, you also need to make sure that you define all the necessary terms before you begin to argue your case. What does it mean to be a "good" society? What makes a novel "feminist"? You should define your terms right up front, in the first paragraph after your introduction.

Second, remember that strong literary essays make contrary and surprising arguments. Try to think outside the box. In the *1984* example above, it seems like the obvious answer would be no, the totalitarian society depicted in Orwell's novel is *not* good for its citizens. But can you think of any arguments for the opposite side? Even if your final assertion is that the novel depicts a cruel, repressive, and therefore harmful society, acknowledging and responding to the counterargument will strengthen your overall case.

5. Write the Introduction

Your introduction sets up the entire essay. It's where you present your topic and articulate the particular issues and questions you'll be addressing. It's also where you, as the writer, introduce yourself to your readers. A persuasive literary essay immediately establishes its writer as a knowledgeable, authoritative figure.

An introduction can vary in length depending on the overall length of the essay, but in a traditional five-paragraph essay it should be no longer than one paragraph. However long it is, your introduction needs to:

- **Provide any necessary context.** Your introduction should situate the reader and let him or her know what to expect. What book are you discussing? Which characters? What topic will you be addressing?

- **Answer the "So what?" question.** Why is this topic important, and why is your particular position on the topic noteworthy? Ideally, your introduction should pique the reader's interest by suggesting how your argument is surprising or otherwise counterintuitive. Literary essays make unexpected connections and reveal less-than-obvious truths.

- **Present your thesis.** This usually happens at or very near the end of your introduction.

- **Indicate the shape of the essay to come.** Your reader should finish reading your introduction with a good sense of the scope of your essay as well as the path you'll take toward proving your thesis. You don't need to spell out every step, but you do need to suggest the organizational pattern you'll be using.

Your introduction should not:

- **Be vague.** Beware of the two killer words in literary analysis: *interesting* and *important*. Of course the work, question, or example is interesting and important—that's why you're writing about it!

- **Open with any grandiose assertions.** Many student readers think that beginning their essays with a flamboyant statement such as, "Since the dawn of time, writers have been fascinated with the topic of free will," makes them sound important and commanding. You know what? It actually sounds pretty amateurish.

- **Wildly praise the work.** Another typical mistake student writers make is extolling the work or author. Your teacher doesn't need to be told that "Shakespeare is perhaps the greatest writer in the English language." You can mention a work's reputation in passing—by referring to *The Adventures of Huckleberry Finn* as "Mark Twain's enduring classic," for example—but don't make a point of bringing it up unless that reputation is key to your argument.

- **Go off-topic.** Keep your introduction streamlined and to the point. Don't feel the need to throw in all kinds of bells and whistles in order to impress your reader—just get to the point as quickly as you can, without skimping on any of the required steps.

---

6. Write the Body Paragraphs

Once you've written your introduction, you'll take the arguments you developed in step 4 and turn them into your body paragraphs. The organization of this middle section of your essay will largely be determined by the argumentative strategy you use, but no matter how you arrange your thoughts, your body paragraphs need to do the following:

- **Begin with a strong topic sentence.** Topic sentences are like signs on a highway: they tell the reader where they are and where they're going. A good topic sentence not only alerts readers to what issue will be discussed in the following paragraph but also gives them a sense of what argument will be made *about* that issue. "Rumor and gossip play an important role in *The Crucible*" isn't a strong topic sentence because it doesn't tell us very much. "The community's constant gossiping creates an environment that allows false accusations to flourish" is a much stronger topic sentence— it not only tells us *what* the paragraph will discuss (gossip) but *how* the paragraph will discuss the topic (by showing how gossip creates a set of conditions that leads to the play's climactic action).

- **Fully and completely develop a single thought.** Don't skip around in your paragraph or try to stuff in too much material. Body paragraphs are like bricks: each individual one needs to be strong and sturdy or the entire structure will collapse. Make sure you have really proven your point before moving on to the next one.

- **Use transitions effectively.** Good literary essay writers know that each paragraph must be clearly and strongly linked to the material around it. Think of each paragraph as a response to the one that precedes it. Use transition words and phrases such as *however, similarly, on the contrary, therefore,* and *furthermore* to indicate what kind of response you're making.

7. WRITE THE CONCLUSION

Just as you used the introduction to ground your readers in the topic before providing your thesis, you'll use the conclusion to quickly summarize the specifics learned thus far and then hint at the broader implications of your topic. A good conclusion will:

- **Do more than simply restate the thesis.** If your thesis argued that *The Catcher in the Rye* can be read as a Christian allegory, don't simply end your essay by saying, "And that is why *The Catcher in the Rye* can be read as a Christian allegory." If you've constructed your arguments well, this kind of statement will just be redundant.

- **Synthesize the arguments, not summarize them.** Similarly, don't repeat the details of your body paragraphs in your conclusion. The reader has already read your essay, and chances are it's not so long that they've forgotten all your points by now.

- **Revisit the "So what?" question.** In your introduction, you made a case for why your topic and position are important. You should close your essay with the same sort of gesture. What do your readers know now that they didn't know before? How will that knowledge help them better appreciate or understand the work overall?

- **Move from the specific to the general.** Your essay has most likely treated a very specific element of the work—a single character, a small set of images, or a particular passage. In your conclusion, try to show how this narrow discussion has wider implications for the work overall. If your essay on *To Kill a Mockingbird* focused on the character of Boo Radley, for example, you might want to include a bit in your conclusion about how he fits into the novel's larger message about childhood, innocence, or family life.

- **Stay relevant.** Your conclusion should suggest new directions of thought, but it shouldn't be treated as an opportunity to pad your essay with all the extra, interesting ideas you came up with during your brainstorming sessions but couldn't fit into the essay proper. Don't attempt to stuff in unrelated queries or too many abstract thoughts.

- **Avoid making overblown closing statements.** A conclusion should open up your highly specific, focused discussion, but it should do so without drawing a sweeping lesson about life or human nature. Making such observations may be part of the point of reading, but it's almost always a mistake in essays, where these observations tend to sound overly dramatic or simply silly.

A+ Essay Checklist

Congratulations! If you've followed all the steps we've outlined above, you should have a solid literary essay to show for all your efforts. What if you've got your sights set on an A+? To write the kind of superlative essay that will be rewarded with a perfect grade, keep the following rubric in mind. These are the qualities that teachers expect to see in a truly A+ essay. How does yours stack up?

- ✓ Demonstrates a thorough understanding of the book
- ✓ Presents an original, compelling argument
- ✓ Thoughtfully analyzes the text's formal elements
- ✓ Uses appropriate and insightful examples
- ✓ Structures ideas in a logical and progressive order
- ✓ Demonstrates a mastery of sentence construction, transitions, grammar, spelling, and word choice

LITERARY ANALYSIS

Suggested Essay Topics

1. *In what sense is* THE GREAT GATSBY *an autobiographical novel? Does Fitzgerald write more of himself into the character of Nick or the character of Gatsby, or are the author's qualities found in both characters?*

2. *How does Gatsby represent the American dream? What does the novel have to say about the condition of the American dream in the 1920s? In what ways do the themes of dreams, wealth, and time relate to each other in the novel's exploration of the idea of America?*

3. *Compare and contrast Gatsby and Tom. How are they alike? How are they different? Given the extremely negative light in which Tom is portrayed throughout the novel, why might Daisy choose to remain with him instead of leaving him for Gatsby?*

A+ Student Essay

What role do automobiles play in *The Great Gatsby*?

For many of Fitzgerald's characters, the automobile represents American progress. Fitzgerald, however, remains unconvinced. Despite its superficial role as an emblem of man's ingenuity, Fitzgerald suggests that the automobile is actually a tool of destruction. Several other symbols of American progress—wealth, scientific research, the metropolis—turn out to be corrupting forces in *The Great Gatsby*. By adding automobiles to this large set of false emblems, Fitzgerald reinforces his idea that the Jazz Age represents a tragic perversion of the American dream.

Several of *Gatsby*'s key players regard automobiles as signs of brilliance and power. Nick marvels at the shiny Rolls Royce that conveys guests to Gatsby's opulent Saturday night parties. Wilson covets Tom's car because it would give him the opportunity to expand his business and improve his social position. Speeding over the Queensborough Bridge in Gatsby's vehicle, Nick feels like an explorer setting eyes on New York for the first time. Again and again, automobiles give Fitzgerald's characters a sense of excitement and possibility.

But Fitzgerald repeatedly shows that these awe-inspiring cars are dangerous, misleading, and destructive. Soon after his wedding, Tom endangers his life by getting into a heavily publicized car accident. (By noting that there is a young female hotel employee in the passenger seat, Fitzgerald suggests that the accident also endangers Tom's marriage.) Leaving Gatsby's party, a drunken buffoon crashes his car and loses a wheel: The man's status symbol exposes him as a weak fool. Though beautiful, Gatsby's leather seats heat up and burn him toward the end of the novel. A speeding car is responsible for Myrtle's death, and Jordan Baker describes her ruined love affair in terms of physical injuries and "bad drivers." The exhilarating joy ride that takes Nick and Gatsby over the Queensborough Bridge ends when a police officer points out that the men are out of control. Fancy cars lead people astray in almost every chapter.

Like the automobile, many other symbols of American prowess prove deceptive in *The Great Gatsby*. Gatsby's parties—celebrated in the papers as pageants of American wealth, style, and genius— turn out to be primitive bacchanals where the guests ignore their host, inebriated men gorge themselves on two dinners, and husbands bicker senselessly with their wives. The scientific report that Tom, the Yale graduate and supposed member of America's intellectual vanguard, brandishes in front of Nick, Daisy, and Jordan turns out to be a barbarous, fictional screed against the global population of non-whites. Nick's move from the Midwest to New York—supposedly an act of bravery and forward thinking—ends in bitterness and disillusionment, not to mention a decision to return to the heartland. Gatsby's self-made wealth comes from racketeering and other shadowy criminal activities. Each emblem of progress and American ingenuity becomes tarnished in this dark novel.

By including the automobile in his array of false status symbols, Fitzgerald calls into question the idea of a wholesome, attainable American dream. The men and women of *Gatsby* set out to spend their wealth in ways that enhance their sense of joy and possibility. Instead, they waste their money on destructive toys, such as powerful cars and huge buffet tables. Fitzgerald's mythic automobile rarely sets his characters on a safe, pleasant path; instead, it injures and kills them.

GLOSSARY OF LITERARY TERMS

ANTAGONIST

The entity that acts to frustrate the goals of the *protagonist*. The antagonist is usually another *character* but may also be a non-human force.

ANTIHERO / ANTIHEROINE

A *protagonist* who is not admirable or who challenges notions of what should be considered admirable.

CHARACTER

A person, animal, or any other thing with a personality that appears in a *narrative*.

CLIMAX

The moment of greatest intensity in a text or the major turning point in the *plot*.

CONFLICT

The central struggle that moves the *plot* forward. The conflict can be the *protagonist*'s struggle against fate, nature, society, or another person.

FIRST-PERSON POINT OF VIEW

A literary style in which the *narrator* tells the story from his or her own *point of view* and refers to himself or herself as "I." The narrator may be an active participant in the story or just an observer.

HERO / HEROINE

The principal *character* in a literary work or *narrative*.

IMAGERY

Language that brings to mind sense-impressions, representing things that can be seen, smelled, heard, tasted, or touched.

MOTIF

A recurring idea, structure, contrast, or device that develops or informs the major *themes* of a work of literature.

NARRATIVE

A story.

NARRATOR

The person (sometimes a *character*) who tells a story; the *voice* assumed by the writer. The narrator and the author of the work of literature are not the same person.

PLOT

The arrangement of the events in a story, including the sequence in which they are told, the relative emphasis they are given, and the causal connections between events.

POINT OF VIEW

The *perspective* that a *narrative* takes toward the events it describes.

PROTAGONIST

The main *character* around whom the story revolves.

SETTING

The location of a *narrative* in time and space. Setting creates mood or atmosphere.

SUBPLOT

A secondary *plot* that is of less importance to the overall story but may serve as a point of contrast or comparison to the main plot.

SYMBOL

An object, *character,* figure, or color that is used to represent an abstract idea or concept. Unlike an *emblem,* a symbol may have different meanings in different contexts.

SYNTAX

The way the words in a piece of writing are put together to form lines, phrases, or clauses; the basic structure of a piece of writing.

THEME

A fundamental and universal idea explored in a literary work.

TONE

The author's attitude toward the subject or *characters* of a story or poem or toward the reader.

VOICE

An author's individual way of using language to reflect his or her own personality and attitudes. An author communicates voice through *tone, diction,* and *syntax.*

LITERARY ANALYSIS

A Note on Plagiarism

Plagiarism—presenting someone else's work as your own—rears its ugly head in many forms. Many students know that copying text without citing it is unacceptable. But some don't realize that even if you're not quoting directly, but instead are paraphrasing or summarizing, *it is plagiarism* unless you cite the source.

Here are the most common forms of plagiarism:

- Using an author's phrases, sentences, or paragraphs without citing the source
- Paraphrasing an author's ideas without citing the source
- Passing off another student's work as your own

How do you steer clear of plagiarism? You should *always* acknowledge all words and ideas that aren't your own by using quotation marks around verbatim text or citations like footnotes and endnotes to note another writer's ideas. For more information on how to give credit when credit is due, ask your teacher for guidance or visit www.sparknotes.com.

REVIEW & RESOURCES

QUIZ

1. Why does Tom hit Myrtle at his apartment in New York City?

    A. Because she refuses to see him anymore
    B. Because she asks him to divorce his wife
    C. Because she taunts him about Daisy
    D. Because she flirts with Nick

2. Where is Gatsby's mansion located?

    A. East Egg
    B. Park Avenue
    C. West Egg
    D. Brooklyn

3. Where does Gatsby's reunion with Daisy take place?

    A. By the pool
    B. At Nick's house
    C. At the golf tournament
    D. At the yacht race

4. In what year is *The Great Gatsby* set?

    A. 1925
    B. 1924
    C. 1923
    D. 1922

5. Where were Nick and Tom educated?

    A. Yale
    B. Harvard
    C. Princeton
    D. Duke

6. What is Jordan Baker's occupation?

   A. Softball pitcher
   B. Secretary
   C. Philanthropist
   D. Golfer

7. When he renews his acquaintance with Daisy at Nick's house, what does Gatsby knock off of the mantle?

   A. Nick's pipe
   B. A clock
   C. Jordan's golf trophy
   D. Daisy's picture

8. What is Nick's home state?

   A. North Dakota
   B. Minnesota
   C. Wisconsin
   D. Florida

9. Why did Gatsby drop out of college?

   A. He had an offer to go into the copper business with Dan Cody.
   B. He and Daisy were getting married, and he needed a job.
   C. He wanted to study Russian, but his college did not offer it.
   D. He was humiliated by having to work as a janitor to pay his tuition.

10. Which millionaire hired the young Gatsby as an assistant?

    A. Cody Baker
    B. Clint McGowan
    C. Hank McGowan
    D. Dan Cody

11. Where is the valley of ashes?

    A.   Between West Egg and New York City
    B.   Between East Egg and West Egg
    C.   Between Death Valley and the Salinas Valley
    D.   Between Greenwich Village and Hell's Kitchen

12. Who among the following comes to Gatsby's funeral?

    A.   Gatsby's father
    B.   Daisy
    C.   Tom
    D.   Klipspringer

13. Which woman is Tom's extramarital lover?

    A.   Daisy
    B.   Ellen
    C.   Myrtle
    D.   Jordan

14. Who drives the car that kills Myrtle?

    A.   Jordan
    B.   Daisy
    C.   Gatsby
    D.   Tom

15. How are Daisy and Nick related?

    A.   They are brother and sister.
    B.   They are married.
    C.   They are step-siblings.
    D.   They are cousins.

16. Where did Daisy meet Gatsby?

    A.   Louisville
    B.   East Egg
    C.   West Egg
    D.   The Plaza Hotel

REVIEW & RESOURCES

17. Where did Gatsby study after the war?

    A. Cambridge
    B. The Sorbonne
    C. Oxford
    D. Yale

18. On the day after the confrontation between Tom and Gatsby in New York City, what does Gatsby instruct his gardener not to do?

    A. Drain the pool
    B. Cut the grass
    C. Rake the leaves
    D. Plant corn

19. At the end of the novel, Daisy chooses to be with

    A. Gatsby
    B. Tom
    C. George Wilson
    D. Nick

20. What are the eyes of Doctor T. J. Eckleburg?

    A. A magazine ad
    B. The lyrics of a song
    C. A painting in the Guggenheim Museum
    D. A signboard in the valley of ashes

21. Why does Nick move to New York?

    A. To become a lawyer
    B. To learn about the bond business
    C. To attend college
    D. To attend medical school

22. What did Fitzgerald call the 1920s?

    A. The Roaring Twenties
    B. The Gay Twenties
    C. The Jazz Age
    D. The Lost Generation

23. Why does Gatsby throw his weekly parties?

    A. To impress Daisy
    B. To cover up his illegal activities
    C. To attract women from East Egg
    D. To impress his neighbors

24. What is Meyer Wolfshiem's claim to fame?

    A. He made the first batch of bootleg alcohol to be sold in New York.
    B. He once beat Al Capone in a fight.
    C. He is a former violinist with the New York Philharmonic.
    D. He rigged the 1919 World Series.

25. Where does Gatsby recognize Nick from?

    A. Nick was an undergraduate at Oxford during the months Gatsby studied there.
    B. Nick works at the bond house where Gatsby's stolen securities were taken from.
    C. Nick and Gatsby fought in the same battle in World War I.
    D. Gatsby has seen his next-door neighbor around, but assumed Nick was one of his own servants.

SUGGESTIONS FOR FURTHER READING

BLOOM, HAROLD, ed. *F. Scott Fitgerald's* THE GREAT GATSBY. New York: Chelsea House Publishers, 2003.

BRUCCOLI, MATTHEW J., ed. *New Essays on* THE GREAT GATSBY. New York: Cambridge University Press, reprint edition 2002.

FITZGERALD, F. SCOTT. *The Letters of F. Scott Fitzgerald.* Ed. Andrew Turnbull. New York: Charles Scribner's Sons, 1963.

————. *Trimalchio: An Early Version of* THE GREAT GATSBY. Ed. James L. West. New York: Cambridge University Press, new edition 2002.

LEHAN, RICHARD D. *F. Scott Fitzgerald and the Craft of Fiction.* Carbondale, IL: Southern Illinois University Press, 1966.

MILFORD, NANCY. *Zelda.* New York: Harper Perennial, reprint edition 2001.

TURNBULL, ANDREW. *Scott Fitzgerald.* New York: Charles Scribner's Sons, 1962.